PIANO · VOCAL · GUITAR

TOP COUNTRY HITS of 2003 2004

WITHDRAWN

ISBN 0-634-07419-9

HAL•LEONARD® CORPORATION
7777 W. BLUEMOUND RD. P.O. BOX 13819 MILWAUKEE, WI 53213

Visit Hal Leonard Online at
www.halleonard.com

CONTENTS

BEER FOR MY HORSES

Words and Music by TOBY KEITH
and SCOTT EMERICK

Moderately, with a beat

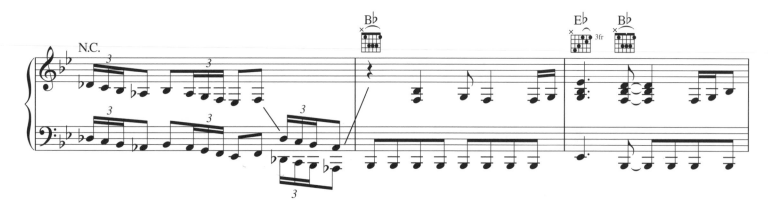

Well, a man ___ come on ___ the

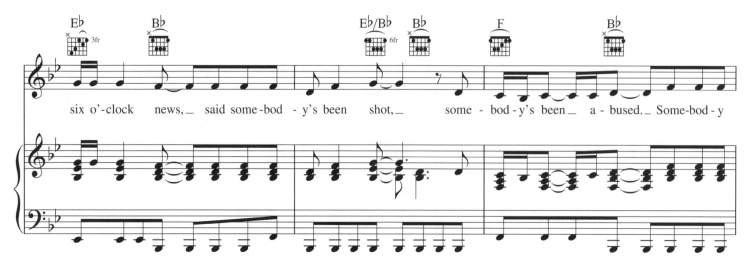

six o'-clock news, ___ said some-bod - y's been shot, ___ some-bod-y's been ___ a-bused. Some-bod-y

blew up a build-ing, some-bod-y stole a car,__ some-bod-y_____ got a-way,__ some-bod-y

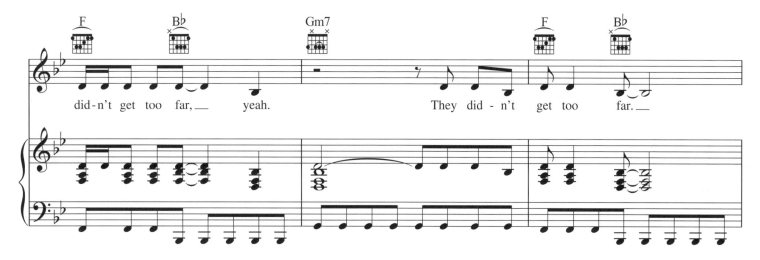

did-n't get too far,__ yeah. They did-n't get too far.__

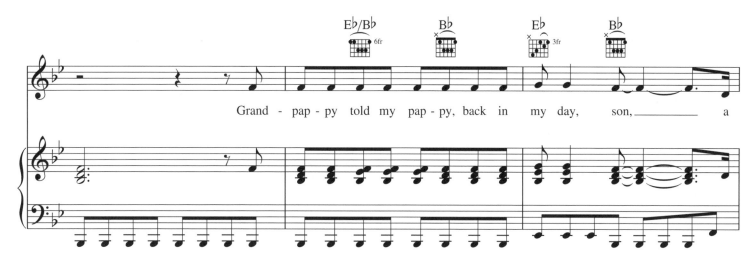

Grand-pap-py told my pap-py, back in my day, son,_____ a

man had to an-swer for the wick-ed that he__ done.__ Take all the rope in Tex-as, find a

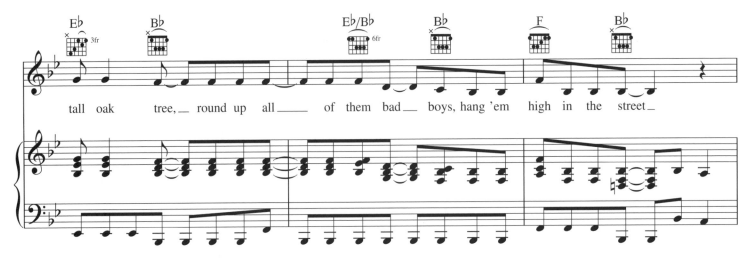

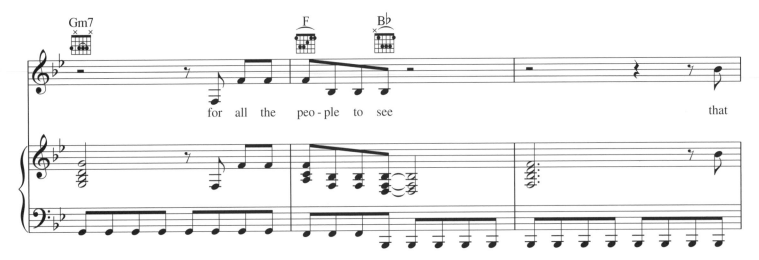

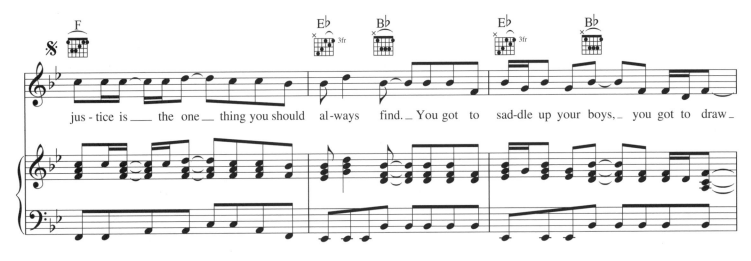

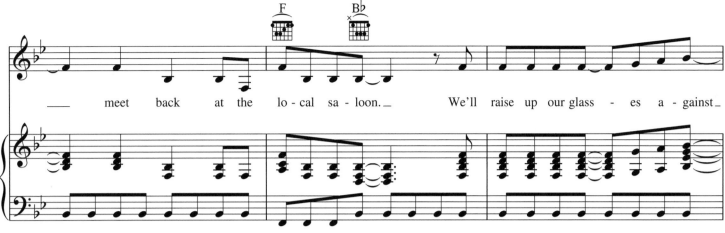

meet back at the lo - cal sa - loon. We'll raise up our glass - es a - gainst

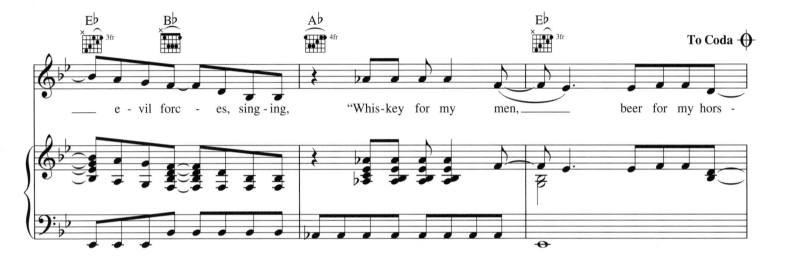

e - vil forc - es, sing - ing, "Whis-key for my men, beer for my hors -

To Coda

- es."

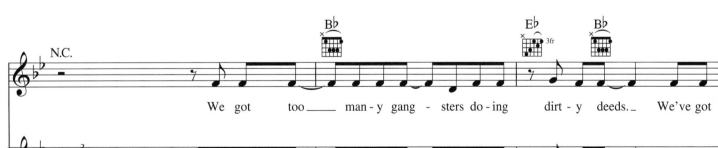

N.C.

We got too man - y gang - sters do - ing dirt - y deeds. We've got

too much cor-rup-tion, too much crime in the streets. __ It's time the long __ arm of the law __ put a

few more in the ground, __ send 'em all to their Mak - er and He'll set-tle 'em down. __

D.S. al Coda

You can bet He'll set 'em down, __ 'cause

CODA

- es, whis-key for my men, __ beer for my
(whis-key for my men)

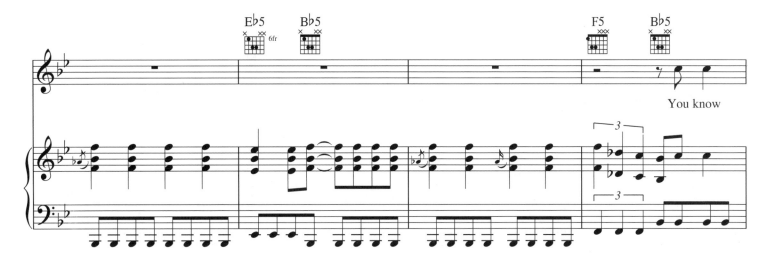

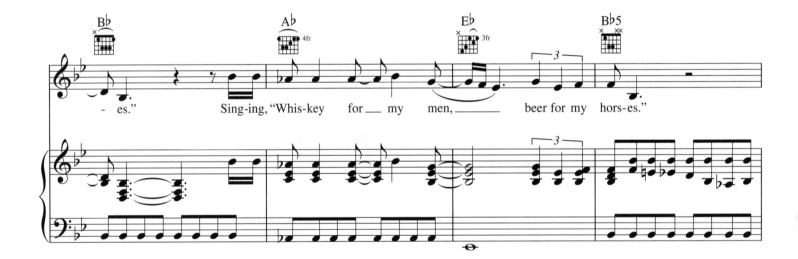

BIG STAR

Words and Music by
STEPHONY SMITH

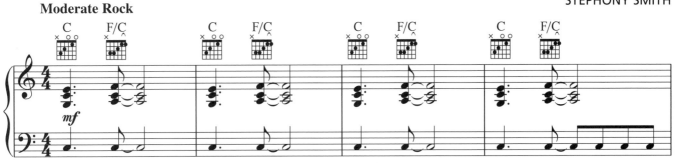

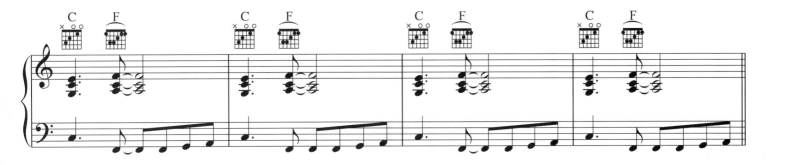

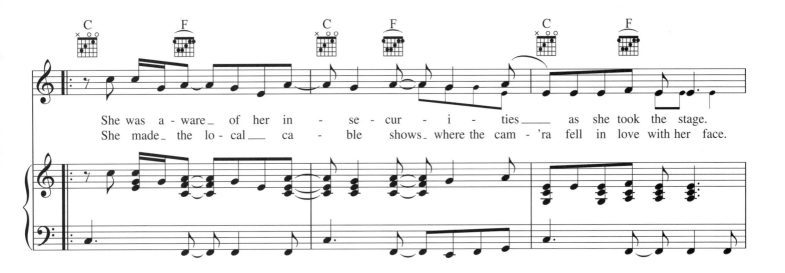

She was a-ware of her in-se-cur-i-ties as she took the stage.
She made the lo-cal ca-ble shows where the cam-'ra fell in love with her face.

She was con-vinced if she got up there, that she'd
Af-ter a cou-ple of week-ends, the group-ies were crawl-

be dis-cov-ered some day. So, she belt-ed it,
in' all o-ver the place. She signed au-to-graphs

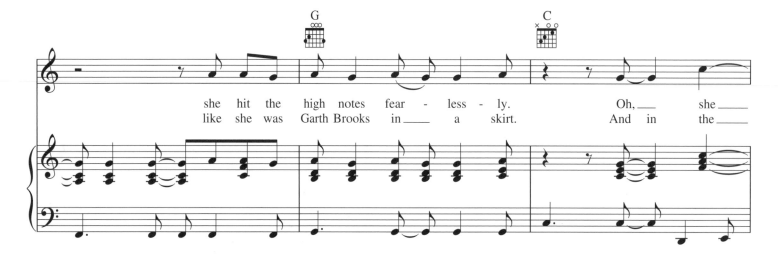

she hit the high notes fear - less - ly. Oh, she
like she was Garth Brooks in a skirt. And in the

melt-ed them. And she brought them to their feet.
af-ter-math, that small-time town was hers.

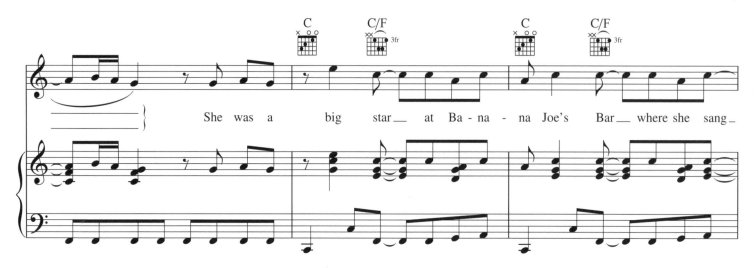

She was a big star at Ba-na-na Joe's Bar where she sang

kar - a - o - ke ev - 'ry night. She said, "If you work hard to get

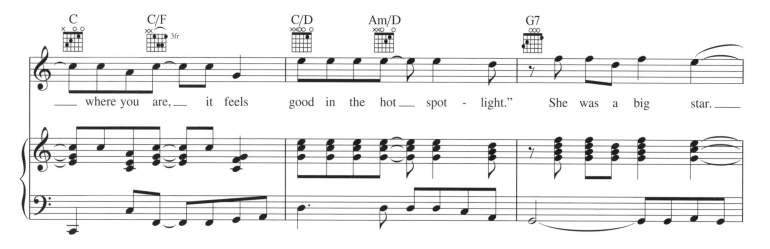

where you are, it feels good in the hot spot - light." She was a big star.

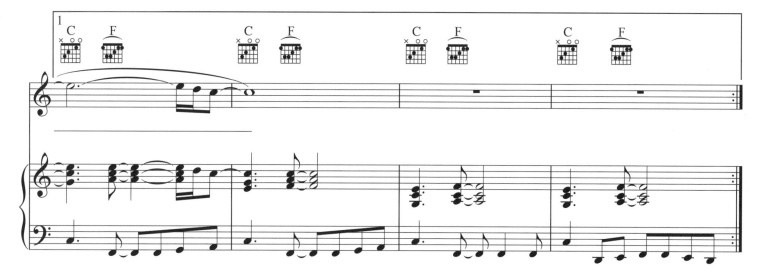

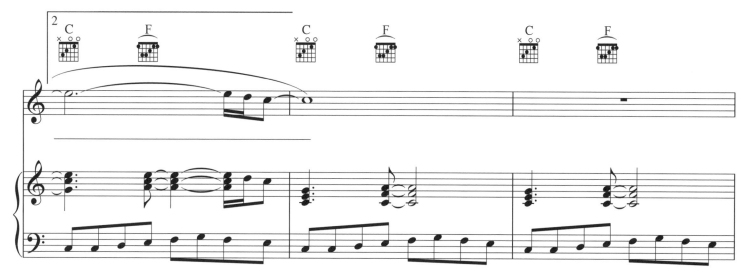

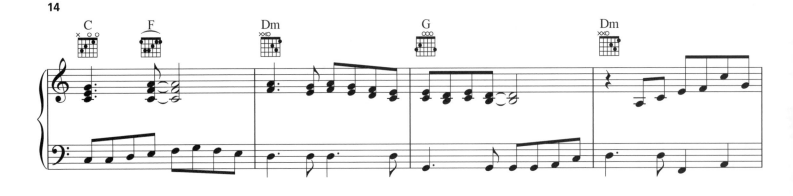

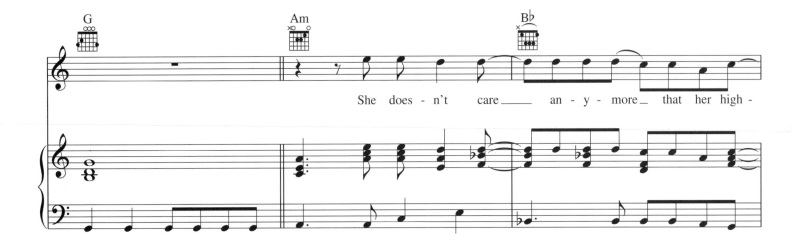

She does-n't care ___ an-y-more ___ that her high-

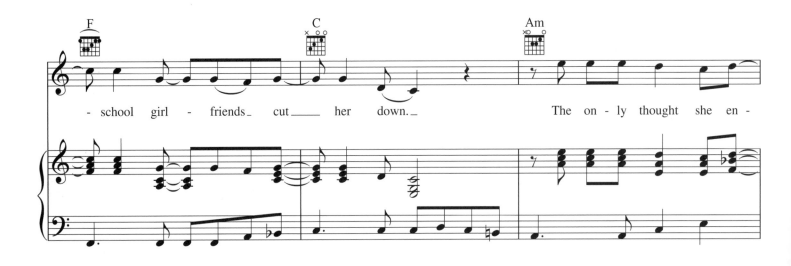

-school girl-friends ___ cut ___ her down. ___ The on-ly thought she en-

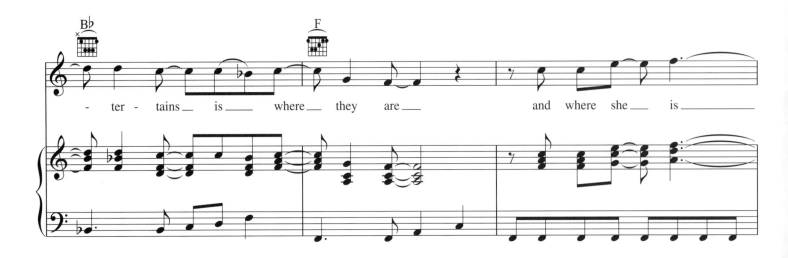

-ter-tains ___ is ___ where ___ they are ___ and where she is ___

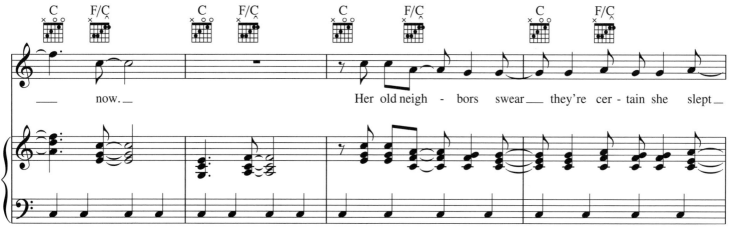

now.____ Her old neigh - bors swear___ they're cer - tain she slept____

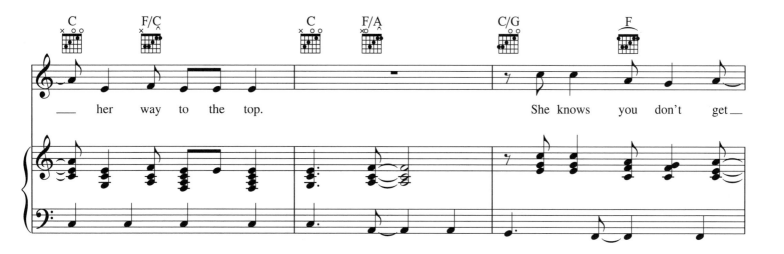

____ her way to the top. She knows you don't get____

____ where you're go - in' 'less you've___ got some - thin' they____ ain't got.____

So, she sings to - night____ to twen - ty - thou - sand plus.

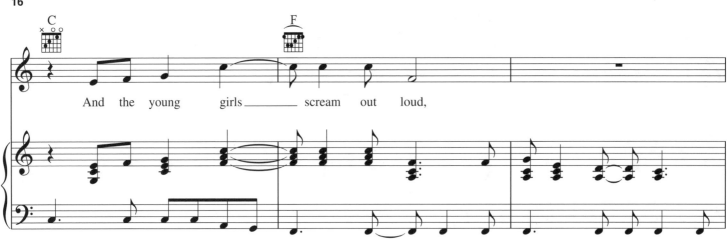

And the young girls _____ scream out loud,

"Man, that could_ be _ us." _____ She's a big star_ as she eats_

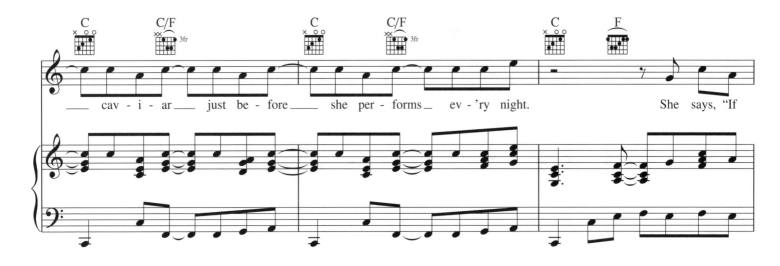

_ cav - i - ar_ just be - fore _____ she per - forms_ ev - 'ry night. She says, "If

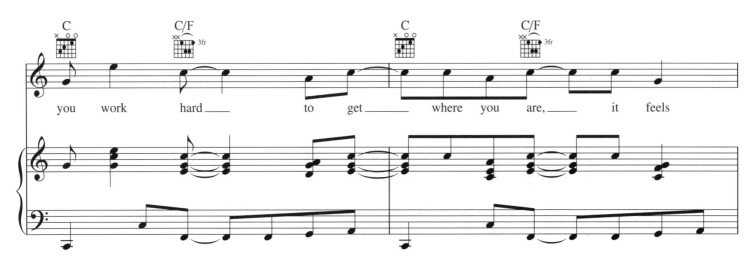

you work hard _____ to get _____ where you are, _____ it feels

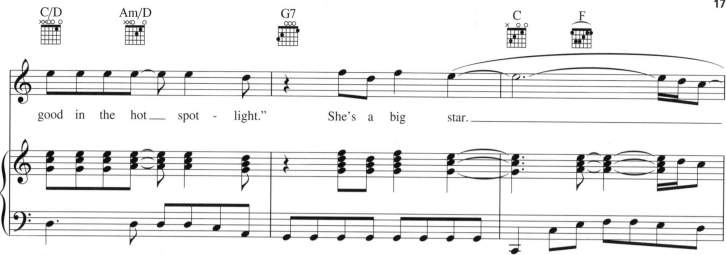

good in the hot __ spot - light." She's a big star. __

__ She's a big star. __

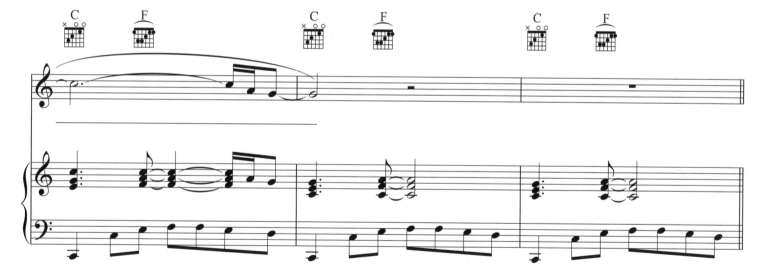

Repeat and Fade

Optional Ending

17

BROKENHEARTSVILLE

Words and Music by DONNY KEES,
CLINT DANIELS, RANDY BOUDREAUX
and BLAKE MEVIS

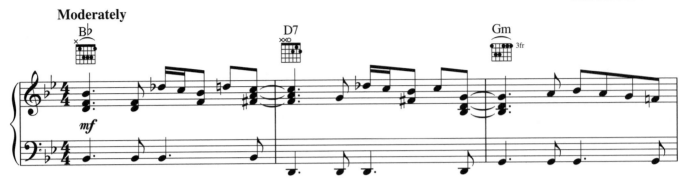

He wore that cow-boy __ hat to cov-er up his horns. __
It was long __ and chrome sit-tin' in the lot, __

Sweet-talk-in' fork-ed tongue __ had a tempt-in' charm. __
fire - en-gine red, __ that __ thing was hot. __

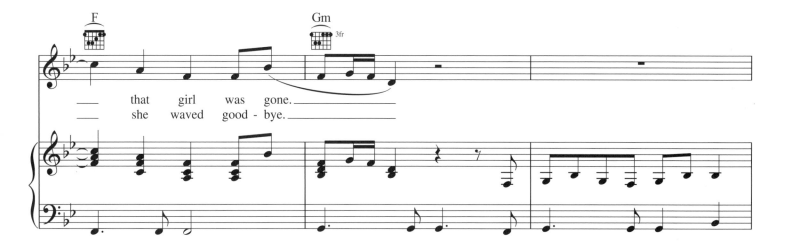

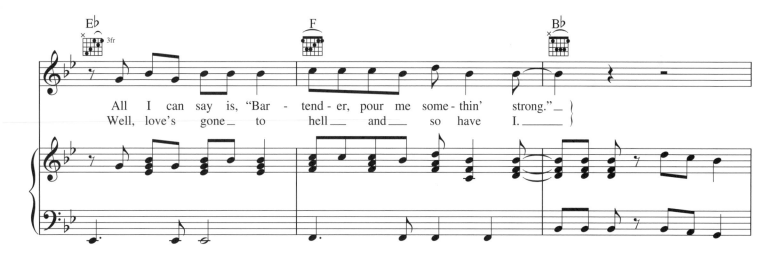

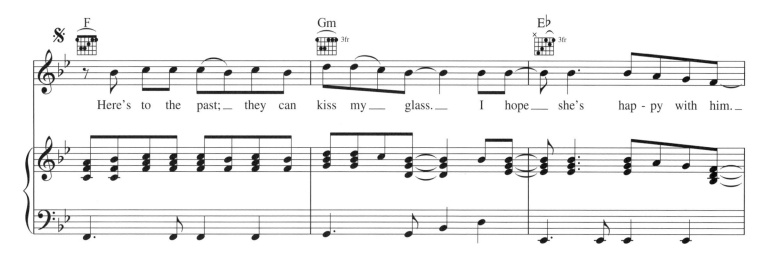

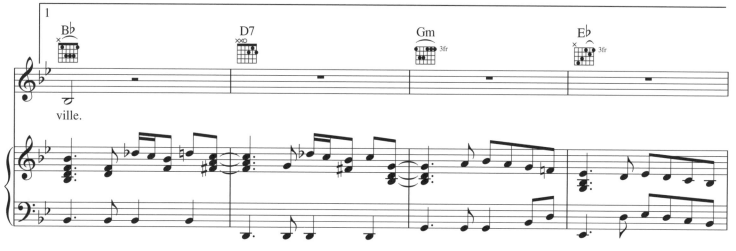

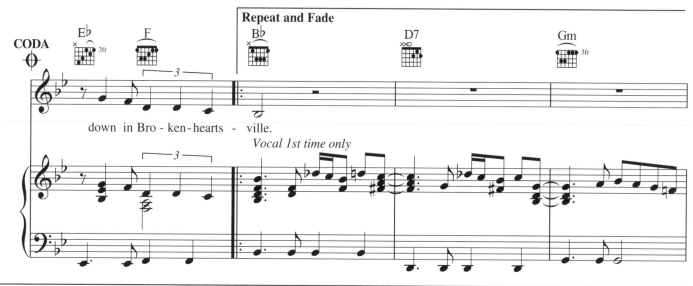

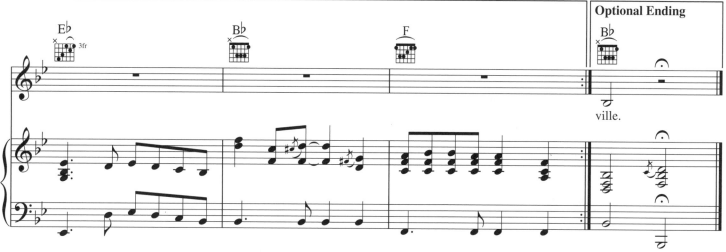

CELEBRITY

Words and Music by
BRAD PAISLEY

Moderately fast

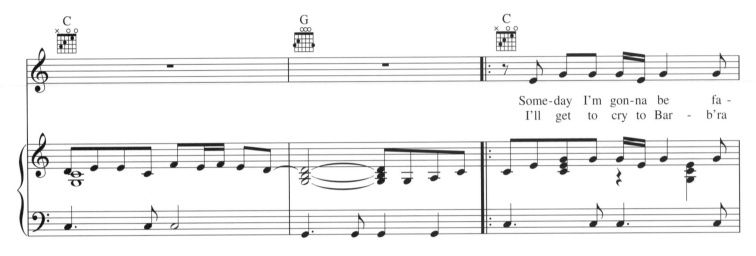

Some-day I'm gon-na be fa-
I'll get to cry to Bar - b'ra

mous.
Wal - ters

Do I have tal - ent? Well, no.
when things don't go my ___ way.

These days you don't real - ly need it ___
And I'll get com-mun - i - ty ser - vice ___

thanks to re - al - i - ty shows.
no mat - ter which law ___ I

Can't wait to date a su-per-mo - del.
break. I'll make the sup - er-mar-ket tab - loids,

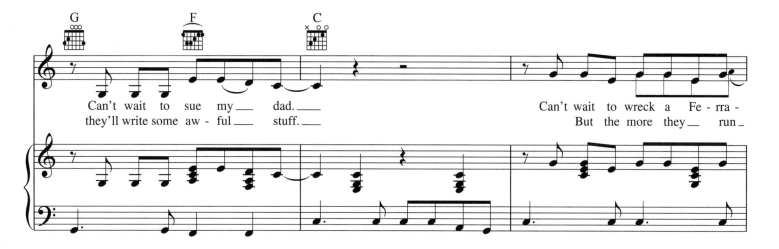

Can't wait to sue my ___ dad. ___ Can't wait to wreck a Fe - rra -
they'll write some aw - ful ___ stuff. ___ But the more they ___ run ___

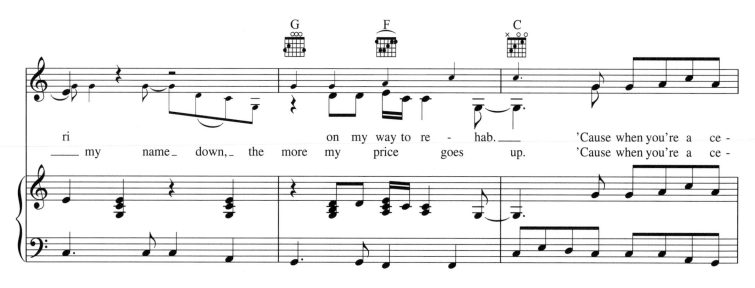

ri on my way to re - hab. ___ 'Cause when you're a ce -
___ my name ___ down, ___ the more my price goes up. 'Cause when you're a ce -

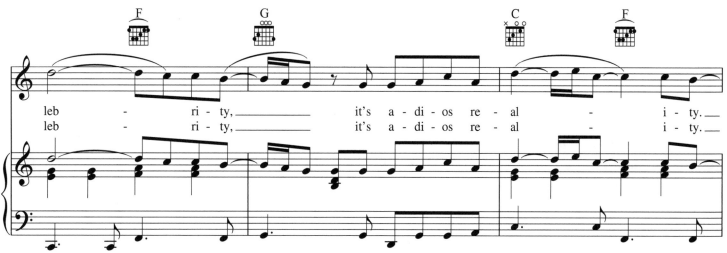

leb - ri - ty, _____ it's a - di - os re - al - i - ty. ___
leb - ri - ty, _____ it's a - di - os re - al - i - ty. ___

You can act just like a fool,__ peo-ple think you're cool__ just 'cause you're on T
No__ mat-ter what you do,__ peo-ple think you're cool__ just 'cause you're on T

V. I can throw a ma - - - jor fit
V. And I can fall__ in and__ out of love,

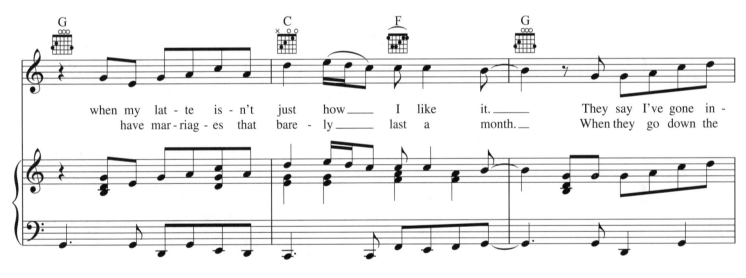

when my lat-te is-n't just how__ I like it.__ They say I've gone in -
have mar-riag-es that bare-ly__ last a month.__ When they go down the

sane.__ I'll blame it on the fame__ and the pres-sures that go__ with }
drain,__ I'll blame it on the fame__ and__ say it's just so__ tough }

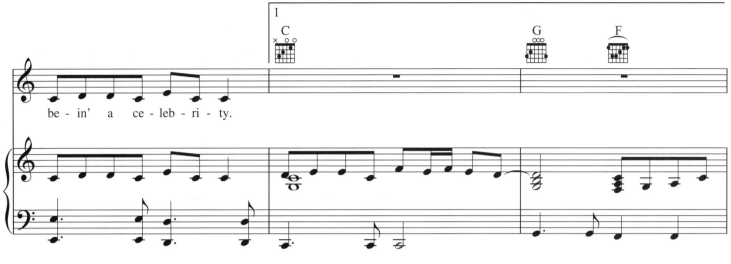

be - in' a ce - leb - ri - ty.

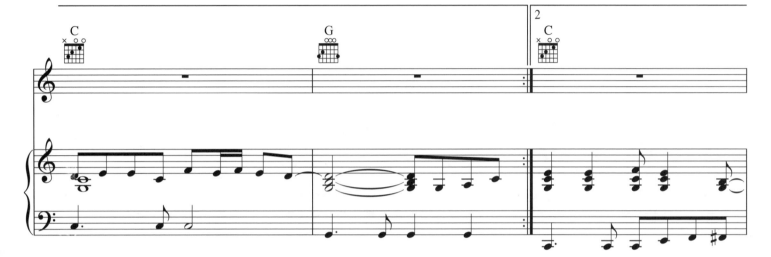

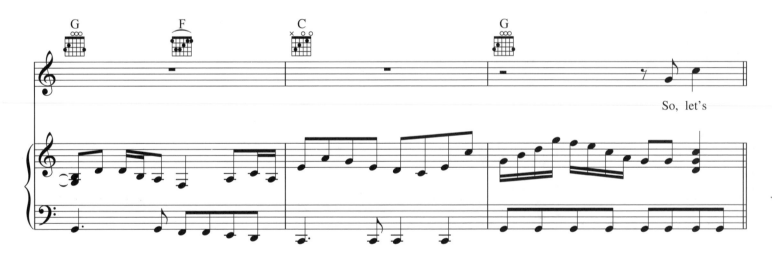

So, let's

hitch up the wag-ons and___ head out___ west___ to the land___ of fun in the

sun. ___ We'll be ___ real world bach - 'lors, Jack - ass mil - lion - aires.

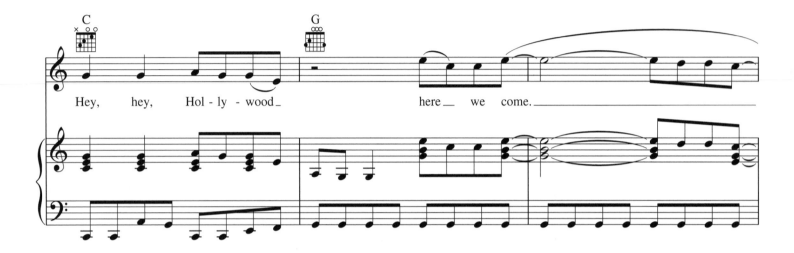

Hey, hey, Hol - ly - wood ___ here ___ we come. ___

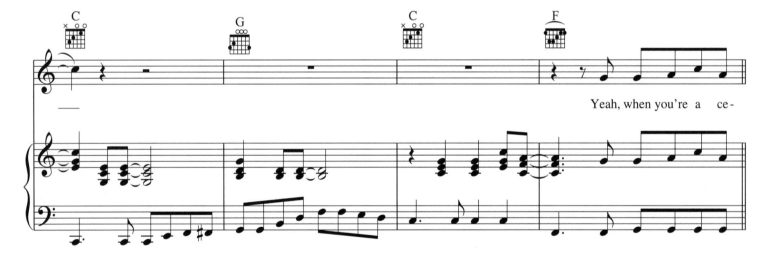

___ Yeah, when you're a ce -

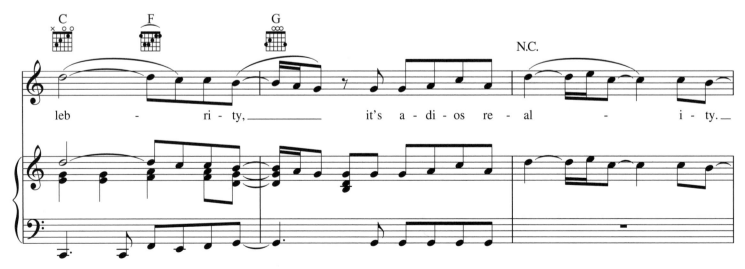

leb - ri - ty, ___ it's a - di - os re - al ___ i - ty. ___

No mat-ter what you do, ___ peo-ple think you're cool ___ just 'cause you're on T

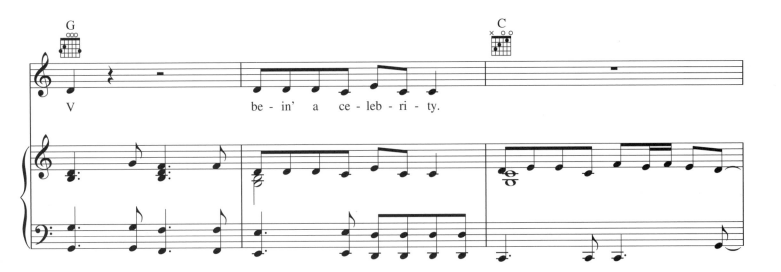

V be-in' a ce-leb-ri-ty.

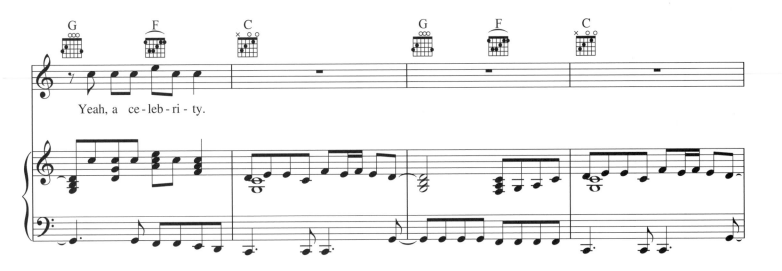

Yeah, a ce-leb-ri-ty.

rit.

COWBOYS LIKE US

Words and Music by BOB DiPIERO
and ANTHONY SMITH

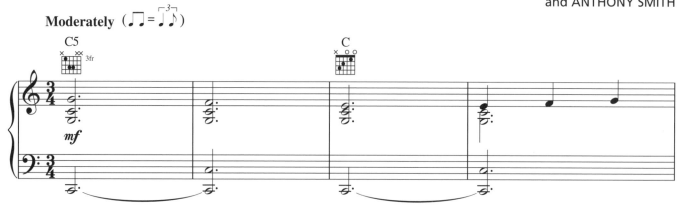

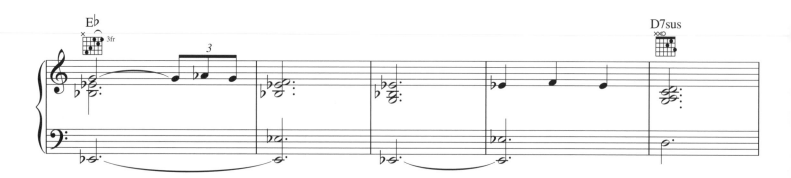

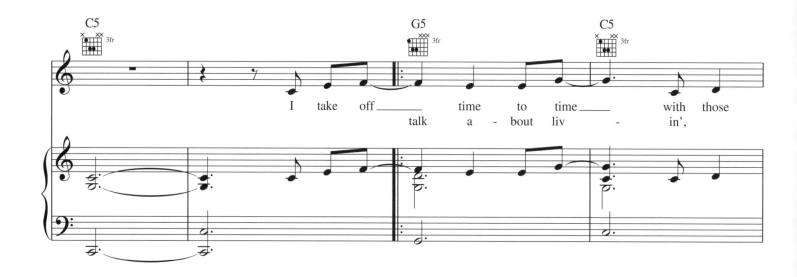

I take off _____ time to time _____ with those

talk a - bout liv - in',

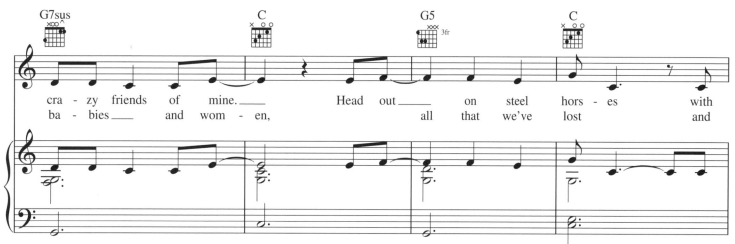

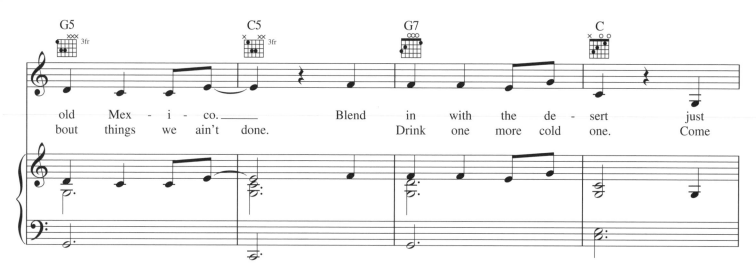

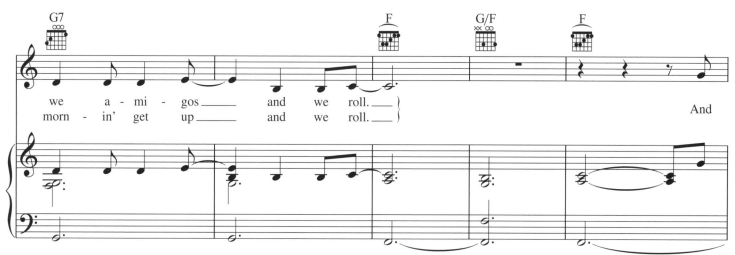

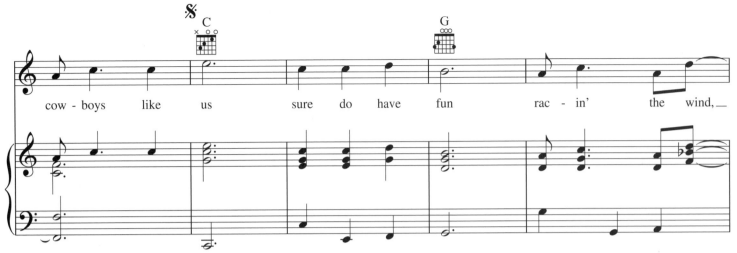

cow - boys like us sure do have fun rac - in' the wind,

chas - in' the sun._____ Take the long way a - round,

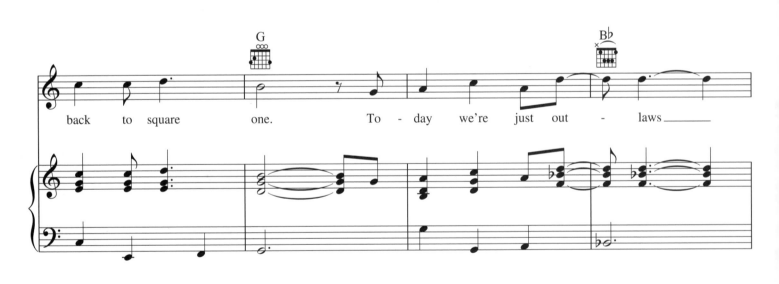

back to square one. To - day we're just out - laws _____

out on the run._____ There'll be no re - grets,_____ no

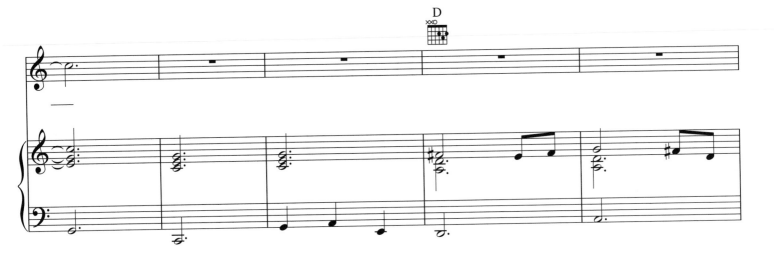

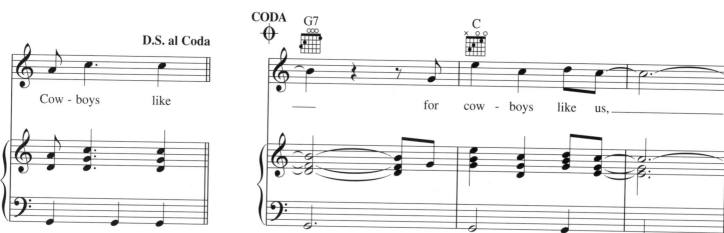

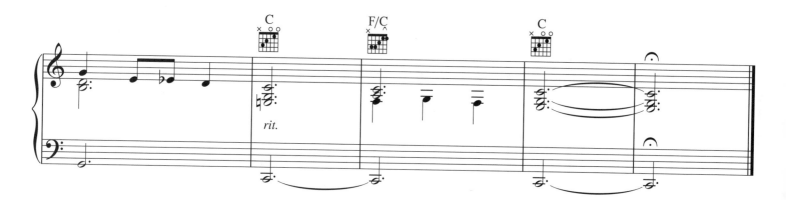

HONESTY
(Write Me a List)

Words and Music by DAVID KENT
and PATTI CLEMENTS

He said, "Just think it o - ver ___ and write me a list, so we can
- ble ___ and placed it in his hand and said, "You

fig - ure out ___ what we both de - serve." She hard - ly could be - lieve ___
know this is - n't eas - y for me," ___ as he thought a - bout the new ___

___ it, that their love had come ___ to this: ___ di -
___ car, the house ___ and ___ the land ___ and

Original key: F# major. This edition has been transposed up one half-step to be more playable.

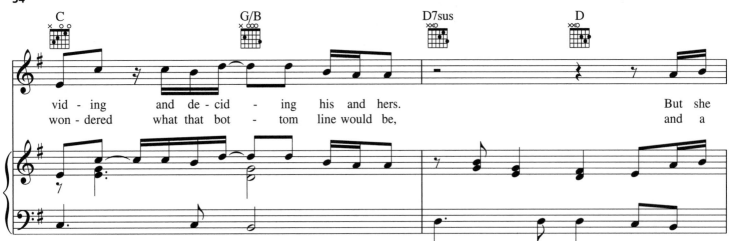

vid - ing and de - cid - ing his and hers.
won - dered what that bot - tom line would be, But she and a

grabbed a pa - per nap - kin, asked the wait - ress for a pen. And one__
thou - sand oth - er things that she'd want him to leave be - hind, but he

__ by one__ she wrote__ down what she want - ed most__ from him.
nev - er dreamed__ he'd o - pen up that nap - kin__ and find

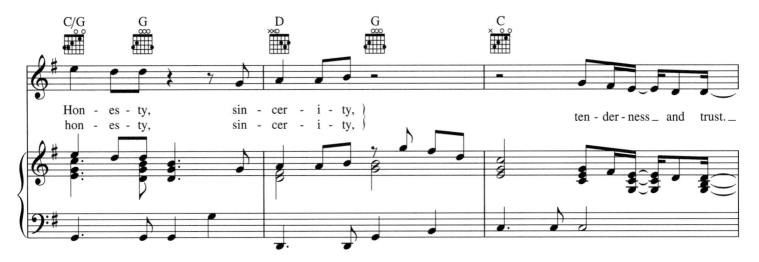

Hon - es - ty, sin - cer - i - ty,
hon - es - ty, sin - cer - i - ty, ten - der - ness__ and trust.__

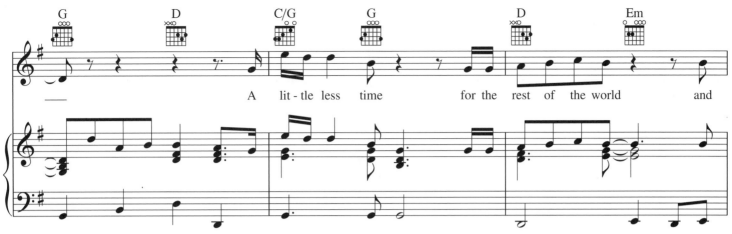

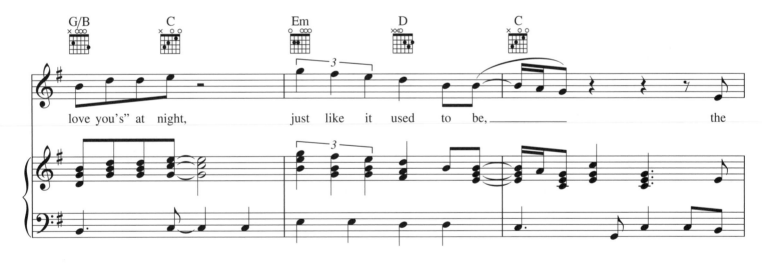

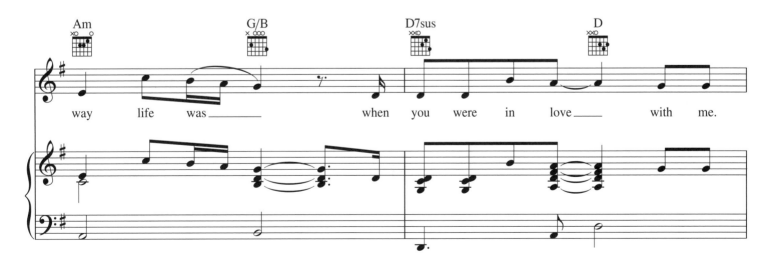

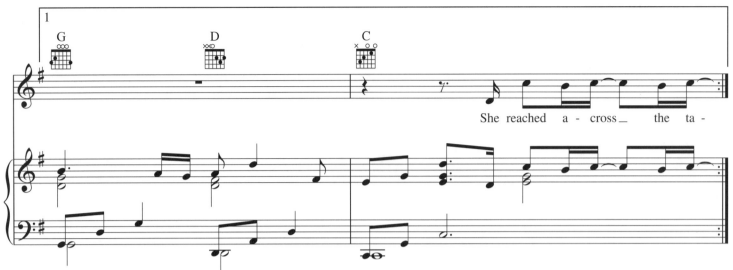

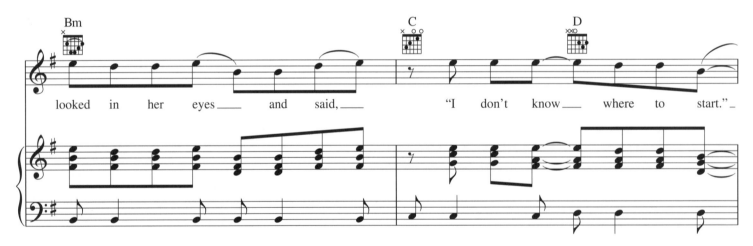

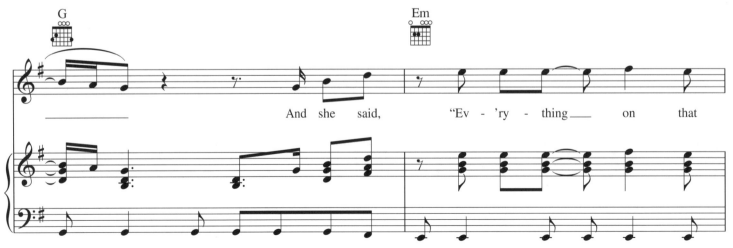

list in your hand ____ is writ-ten some-where in ____ your heart." ____

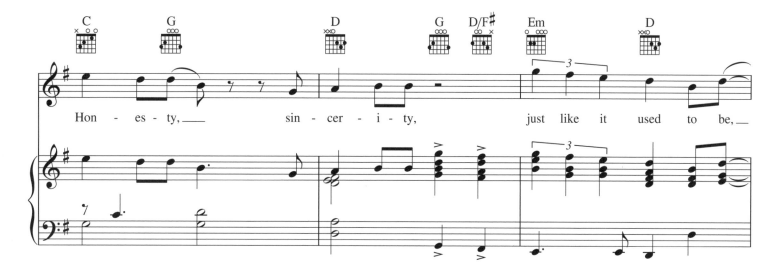

Hon - es - ty, ____ sin - cer - i - ty, just like it used to be, ___

the way life ___ was ___ when you were in love ___

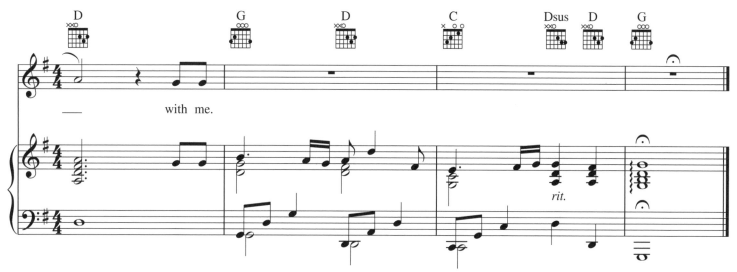

___ with me.

HAVE YOU FORGOTTEN?

Words and Music by DARRYL WORLEY
and WYNN VARBLE

I hear peo-ple say-in' we don't need this war.
They took all the foot-age off my T V.

But I say there's some____ things worth fight-in' for.
Said it's too dis-turb-ing for you and me.

Play 1st time only

you this, ___ my friend: _____ Have you for - got - ten
to say ___ that's right. _____

(1.,2.) how it felt ___ that day, ___ to see your home - land ___ un - der fire ___
(D.S.) - ple killed? ___ Yes, some ___ went ___ down like he -

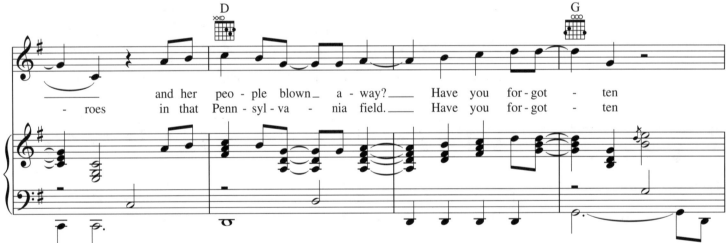

and her peo - ple blown ___ a - way? ___ Have you for - got - ten
- roes in that Penn - syl - va - nia field. ___ Have you for - got - ten

when those tow - ers fell? _____ We had neigh - bors still in - side,
a - bout our Pen - ta - gon? All the loved ___ ones that we lost ___

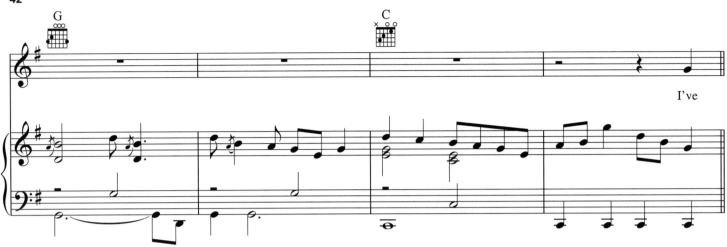

I've

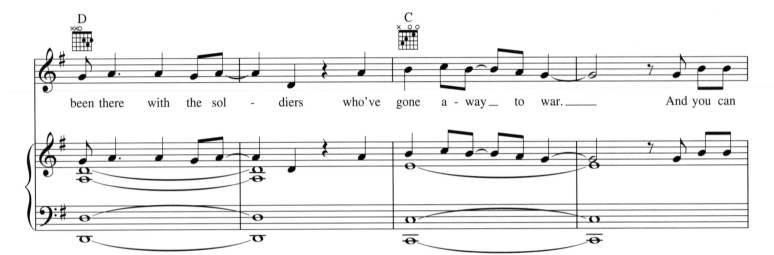

been there with the sol - diers who've gone a - way_ to war._ And you can

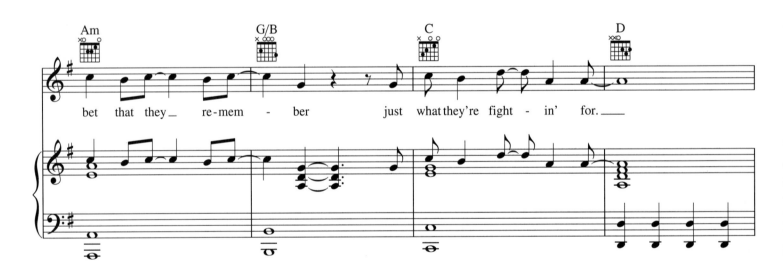

bet that they_ re-mem - ber just what they're fight - in' for._

D.S. al Coda

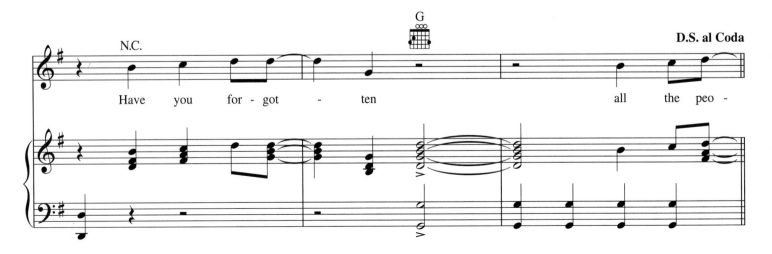

N.C.

Have you for-got - ten all the peo -

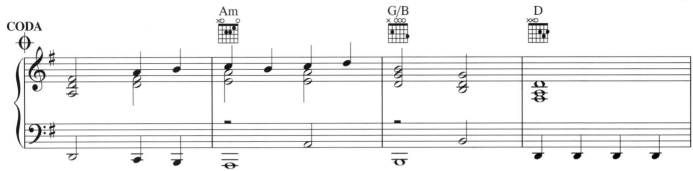

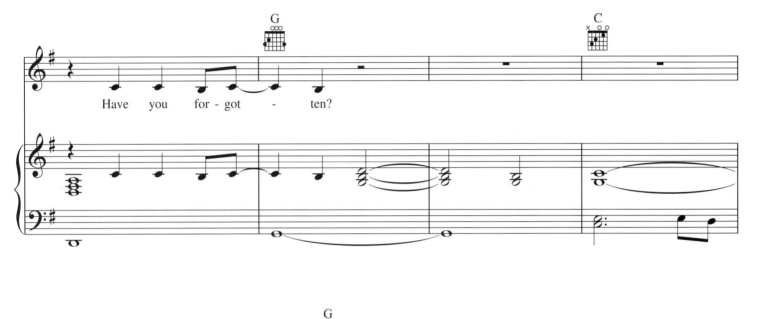

Have you for-got - ten?

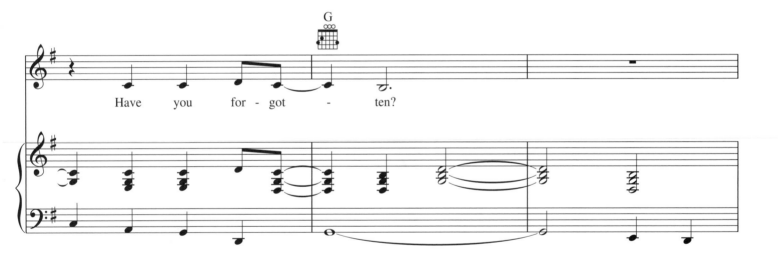

Have you for got - ten?

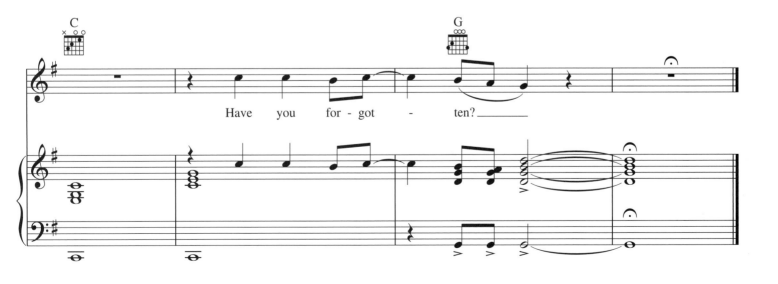

Have you for-got - ten?

I BELIEVE

Words and Music by SKIP EWING
and DONNY KEES

Slowly, with feeling

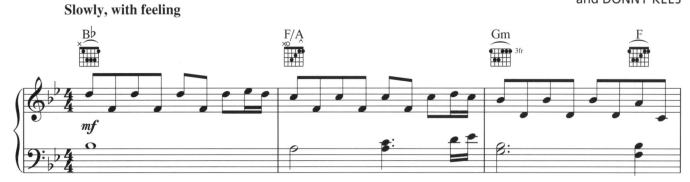

Ev-'ry now _ and then, soft as breath _ up-on _ my skin, _ I feel _

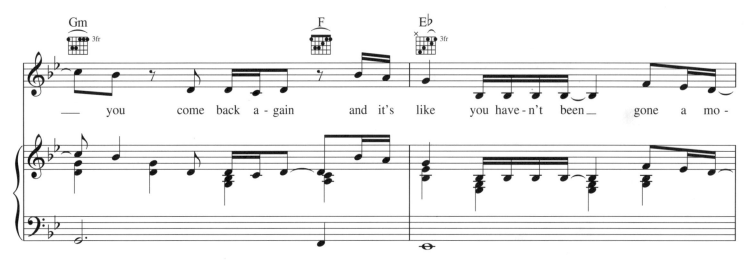

_ you come back a-gain and it's like you have-n't been _ gone a mo-

-ment from _ my side. _ Like the tears _ were nev-er cried. Like the hands _

of time___ are hold - ing you___ and me.___ And with

all my heart___ I'm sure we're clos - er than we ev - er were. I don't___ have___

to hear__ or see. I've got__ all____ the proof__ I need. There__ are more__

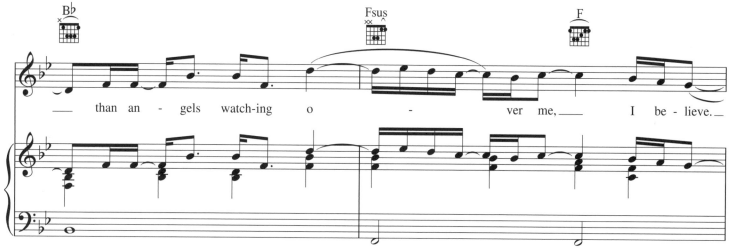

than an - gels watch-ing o - ver me,___ I be - lieve.___

Oh, I be - lieve.____ Now when you

die your life __ goes on. It does - n't end ____ here when you're gone.____ Ev - 'ry soul __

__ is filled __ with light. It nev - er ends, ____ if I'm right. Our __ love can

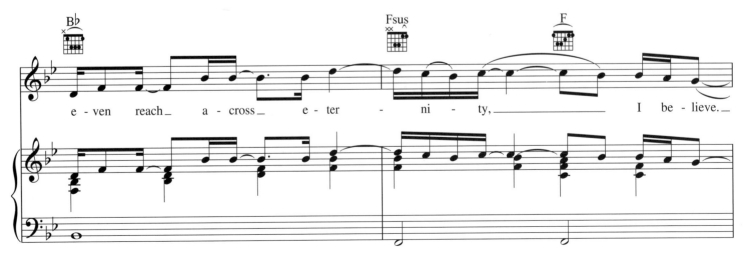

e - ven reach __ a - cross ____ e - ter - ni - ty, _____ I be - lieve. __

Oh, I be - lieve.___

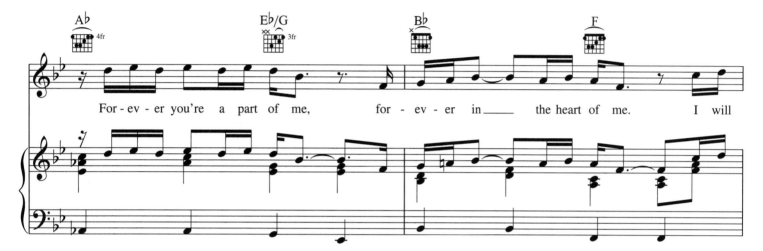

For - ev - er you're a part of me, for - ev - er in___ the heart of me. I will

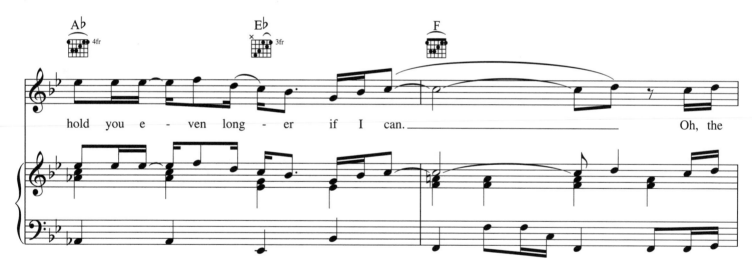

hold you e - ven long - er if I can.___ Oh, the

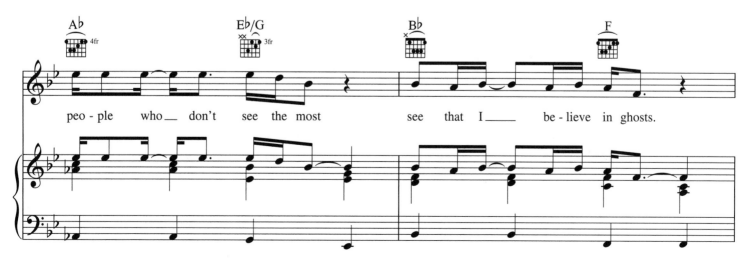

peo - ple who__ don't see the most see that I___ be - lieve in ghosts.

If that makes_ me cra - zy, then I am _____ 'cause I be - lieve.

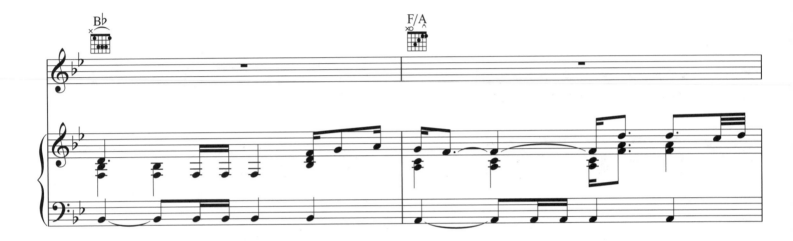

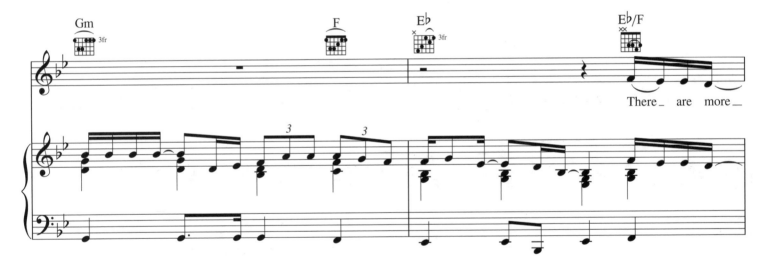

There_ are more_

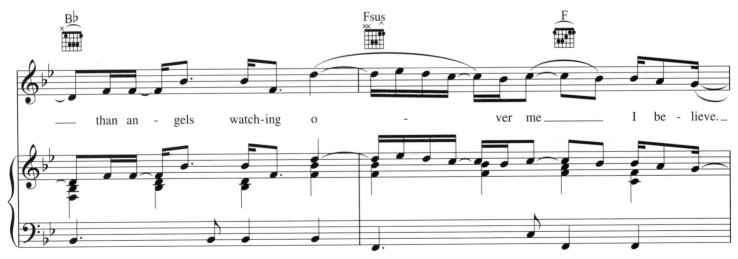

___ than an - gels watch-ing o - ver me _____ I be - lieve._

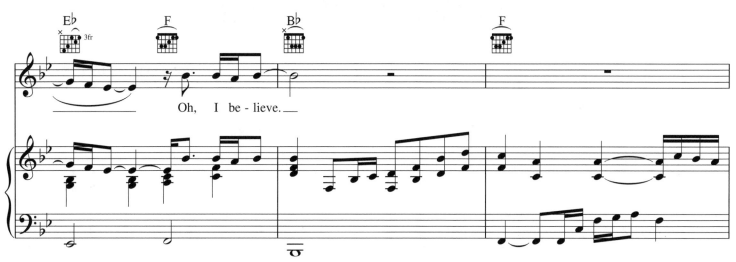

Oh, I be - lieve.

Ev - 'ry now and then soft as breath

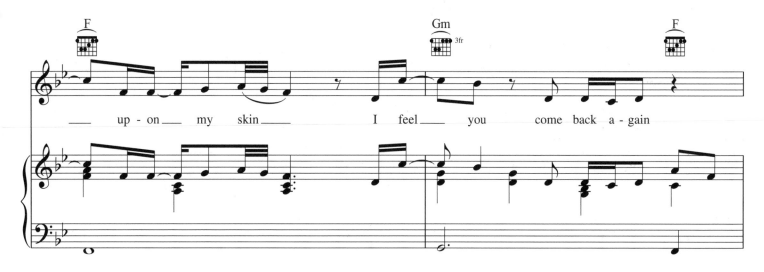

up - on my skin I feel you come back a - gain

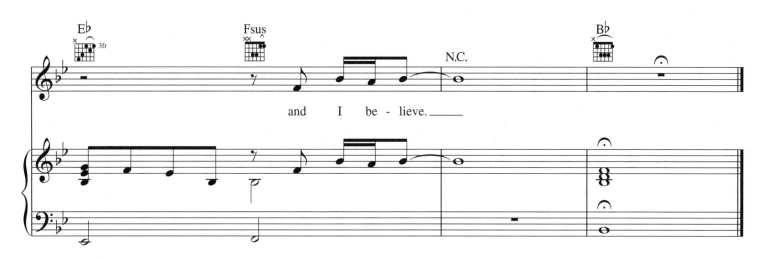

and I be - lieve.

I LOVE THIS BAR

Words and Music by TOBY KEITH
and SCOTT EMERICK

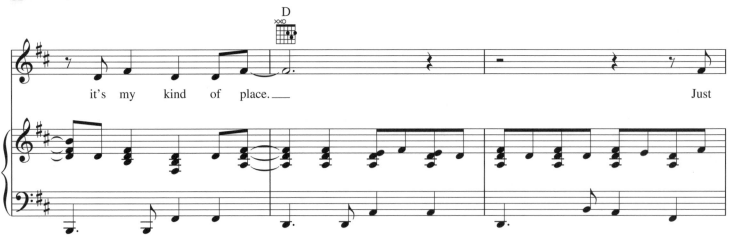

it's my kind of place.___ Just

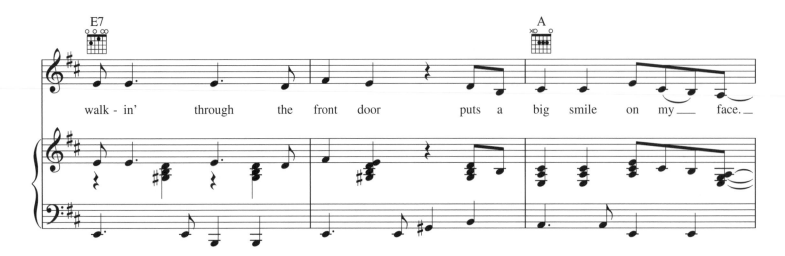

walk - in' through the front door puts a big smile on my ___ face.___

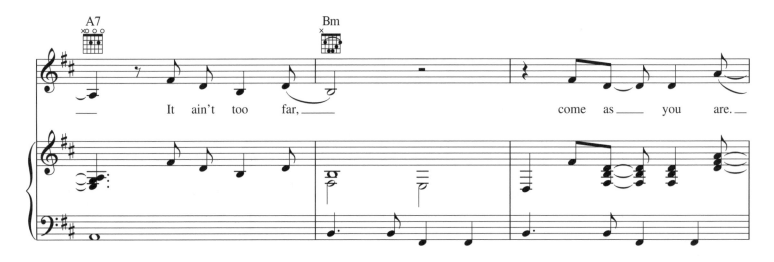

___ It ain't too far, ___ come as ___ you are. ___

Hmm, ___ hmm, ___

D.S. al Coda

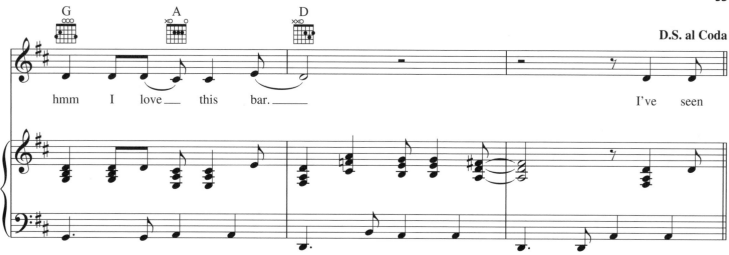

hmm I love ___ this bar. ___

I've seen

CODA

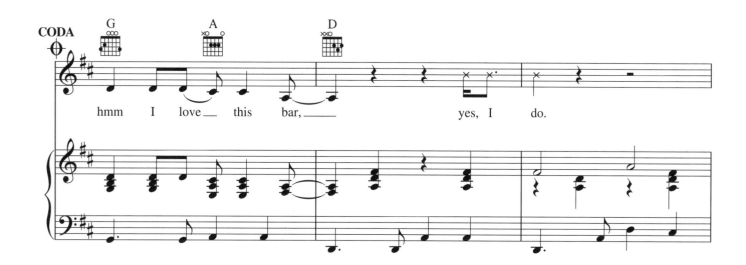

hmm I love ___ this bar, ___

yes, I do.

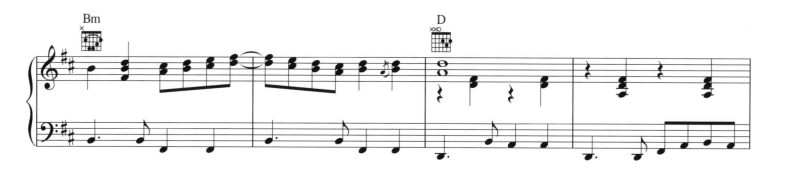

I like ___ my ___ truck, ___

I like __ my __ girl - friend. __ I like to

take her out __ to din - ner. I like a mov - ie now __ and then.

But I love this bar, it's my kind __ of place. __

Just troll - in' a - round __ the dance floor puts a big smile on my __ face. __

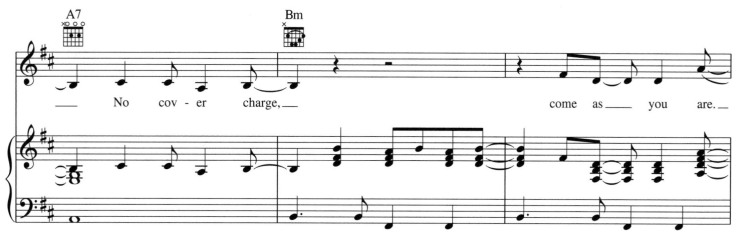

No cov-er charge, ___ come as ___ you are. ___

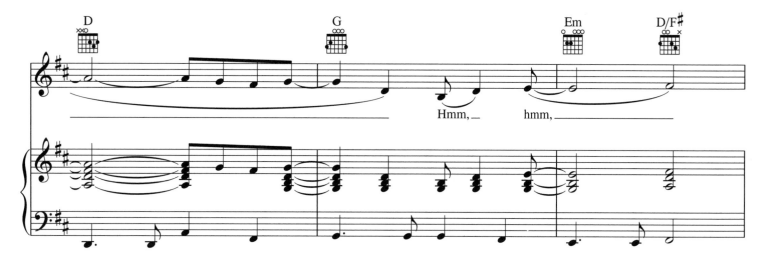

Hmm, ___ hmm, ___

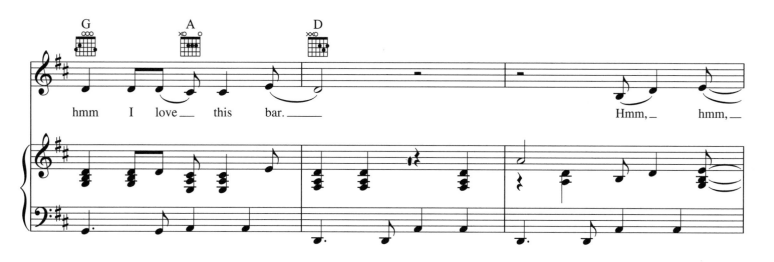

hmm I love ___ this bar. ___ Hmm, ___ hmm, ___

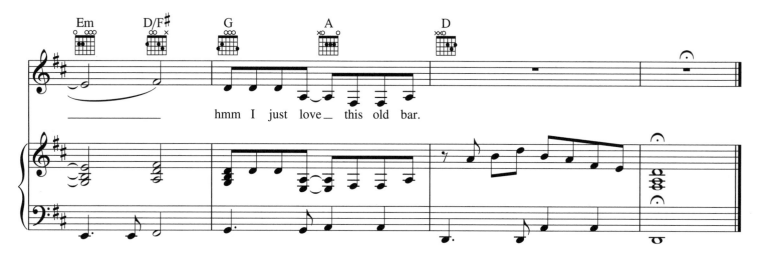

___ hmm I just love ___ this old bar.

I MELT

Words and Music by GARY LEVOX,
WENDELL MOBLEY and NEIL THRASHER

Moderately slow

When you light those can - dles
Don't know how you do ____ it. ____

up there ____ on that man - tle, set - tin' the mood, ____
I love the way I ____ lose ____ it ev - er - y time. ____

Ain't it wild what a lit-tle flame ___ can make you ___ want to do? ___
One ___ lit-tle stare from you, ___ is ___ all ___ it takes. ___

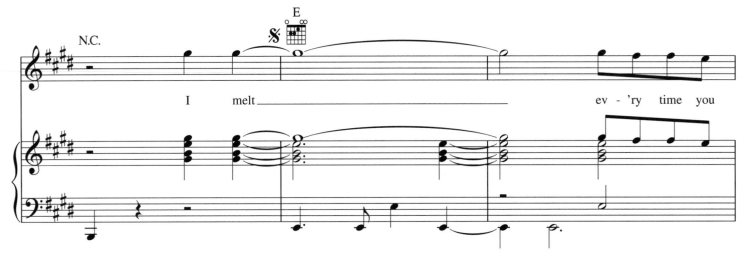

I melt ___ ev-'ry time you

look at me that - a way. It nev - er fails ___

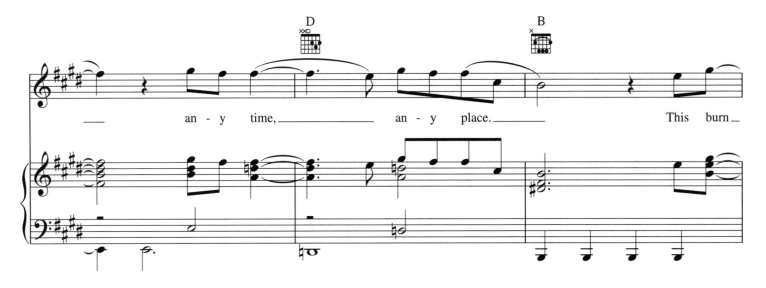

___ an - y time, ___ an - y place. ___ This burn ___

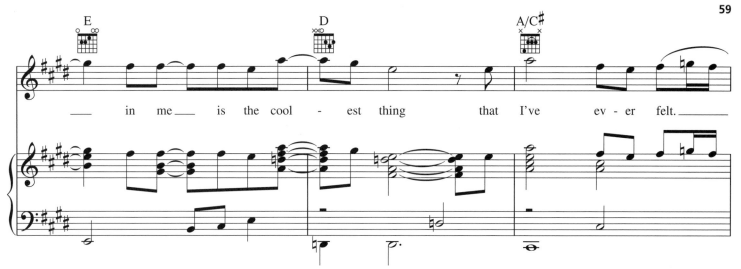

in me __ is the cool - est thing that I've ev - er felt. __

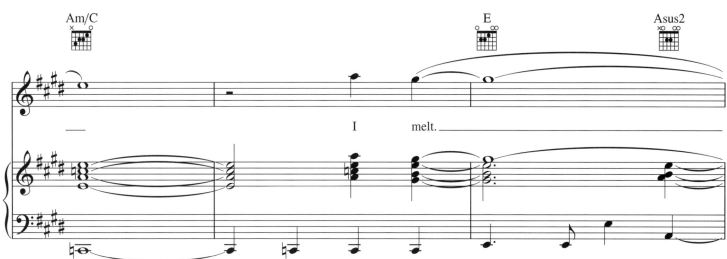

I melt. __

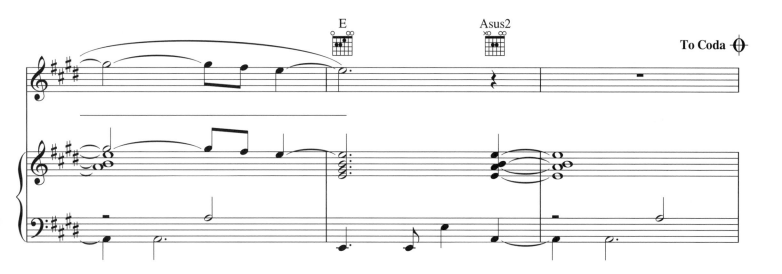

To Coda ⊕

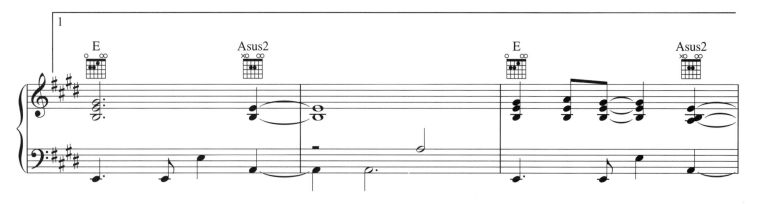

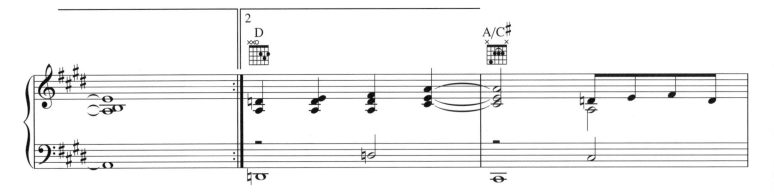

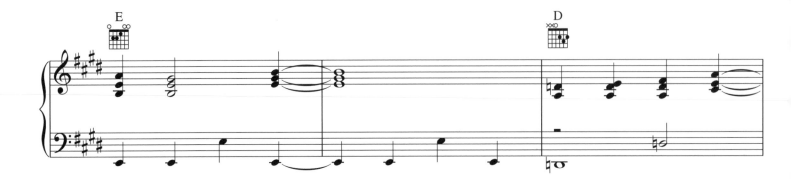

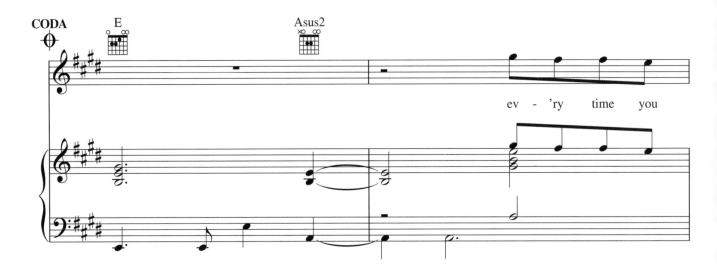

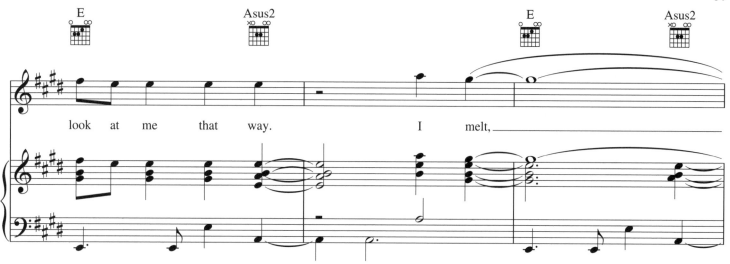

look at me that way. I melt,

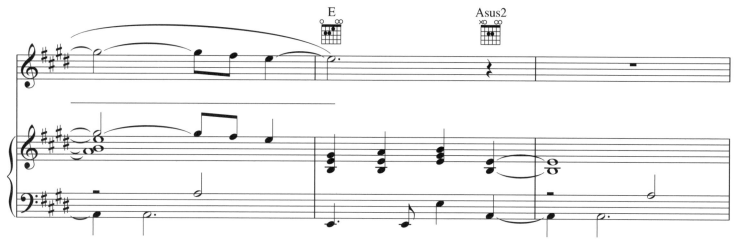

I melt.

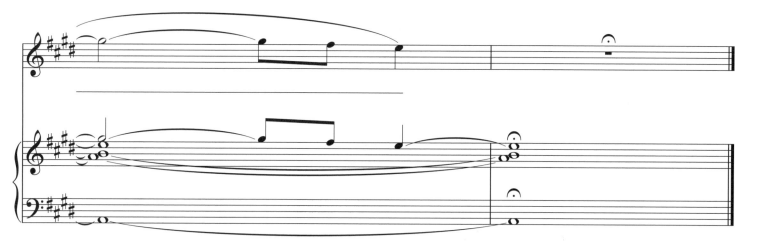

I WISH

Words and Music by ED HILL
and TOMMY LEE JAMES

Moderately slow

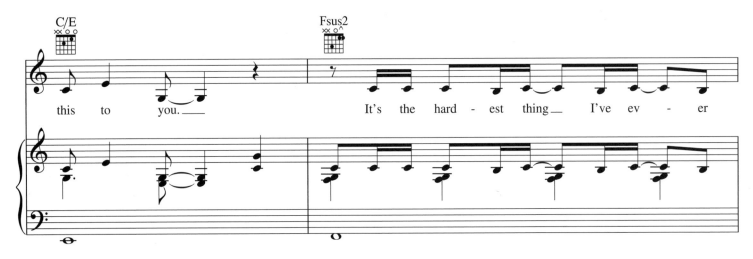

It's not eas - y say - in'

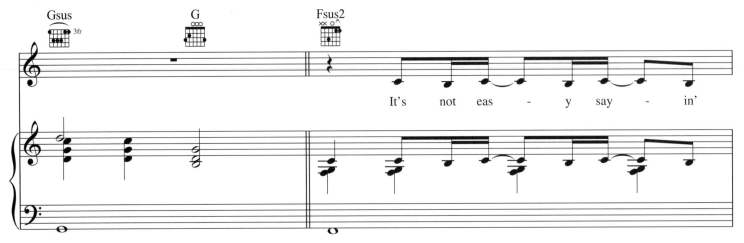

this to you.___ It's the hard - est thing___ I've ev - er

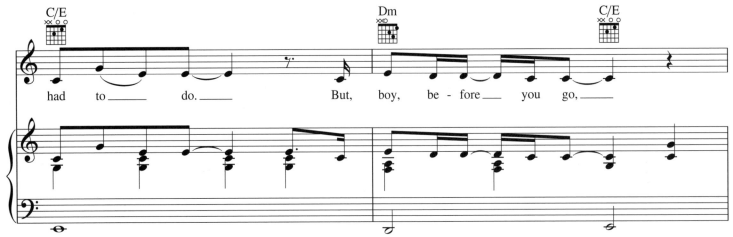

had to ___ do. ___ But, boy, be - fore ___ you go, ___

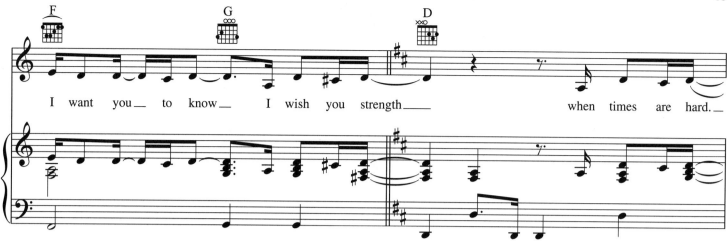

I want you to know__ I wish you strength____ when times are hard.__

Oh, I wish__ with all__ my heart____ you'll find__ just what__

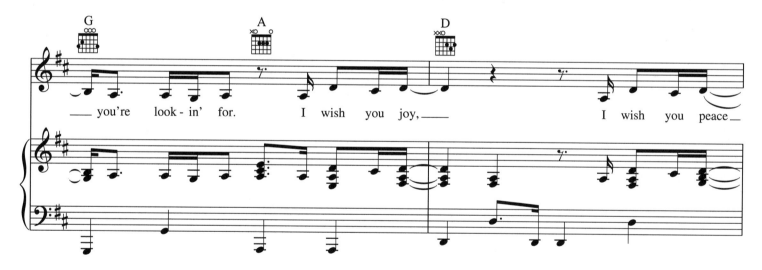

__ you're look-in' for. I wish you joy,____ I wish you peace__

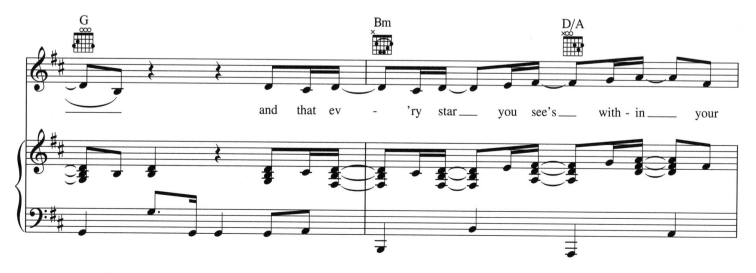

and that ev - 'ry star__ you see's__ with - in____ your

reach. And I wish you still _____ loved ___ me. ___

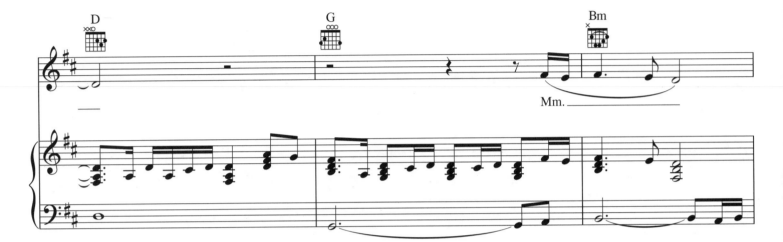

___ Mm. _____

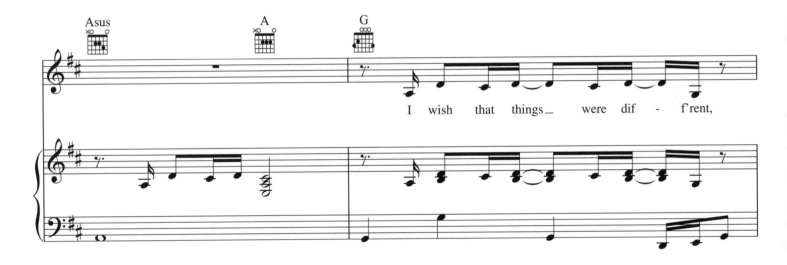

I wish that things ___ were dif - f'rent,

you know that. But I'm still hap - py for _____ the times ___

we __ had. __ You mean the world __ to me. __ Oh, ba-

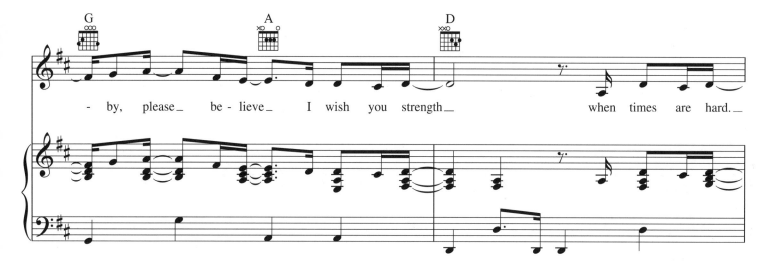

-by, please __ be - lieve __ I wish you strength __ when times are hard. __

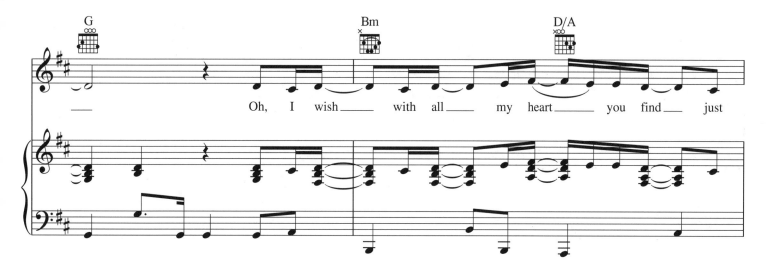

__ Oh, I wish __ with all __ my heart __ you find __ just

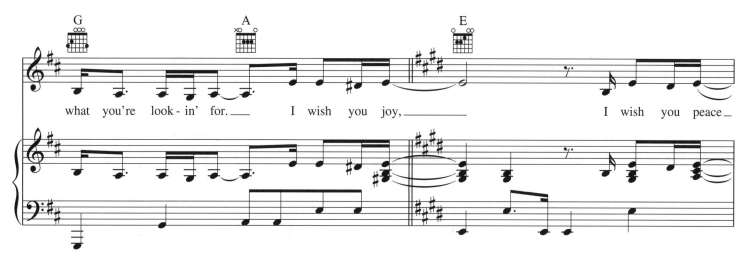

what you're look - in' for. __ I wish you joy, __ I wish you peace __

and that ev - 'ry star___ you see's___ with - in___ your

reach.___ And I wish___ you still___ loved me.___ Oh,___

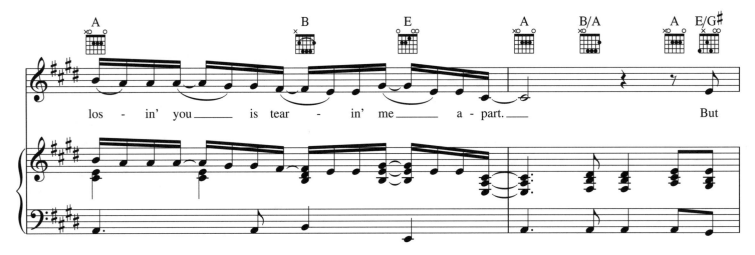

los - in' you___ is tear - in' me___ a - part.___ But

part___ of me___ will be___ with you___ no mat - ter where___ you are.___

68

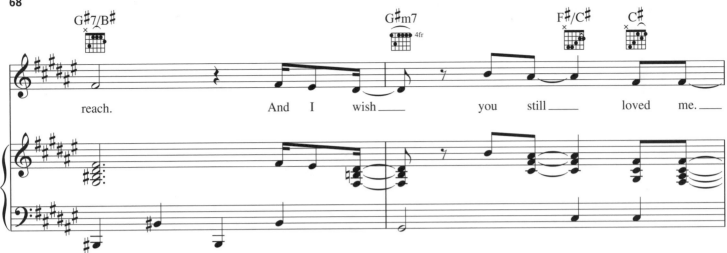

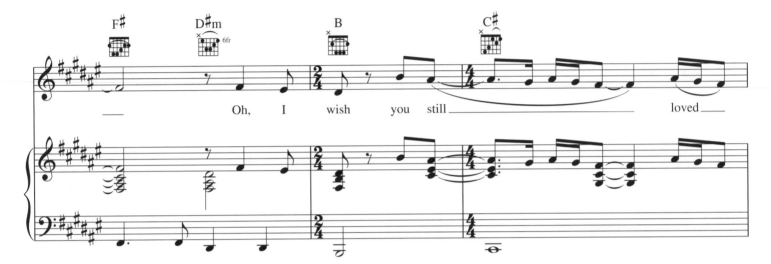

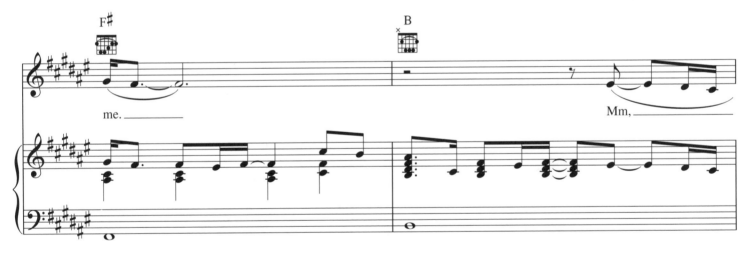

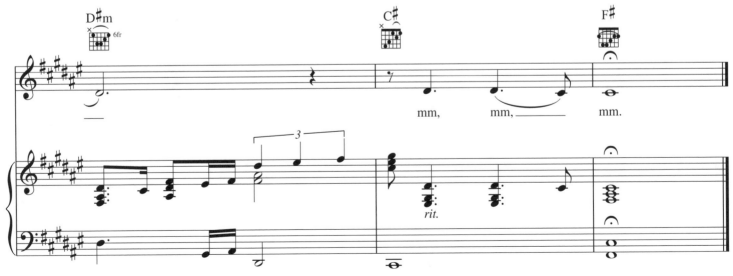

MY FRONT PORCH LOOKING IN

Words and Music by RICHIE McDONALD,
FRANK MYERS and DON PFRIMMER

Moderately fast, in 2

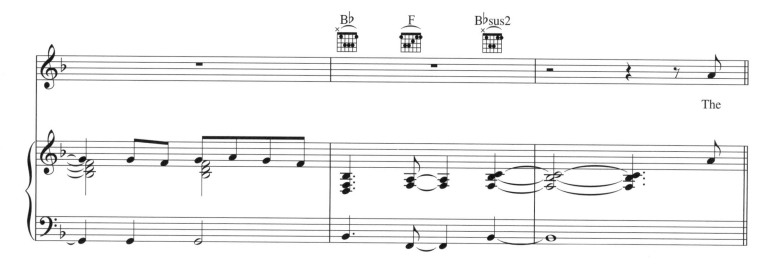

The

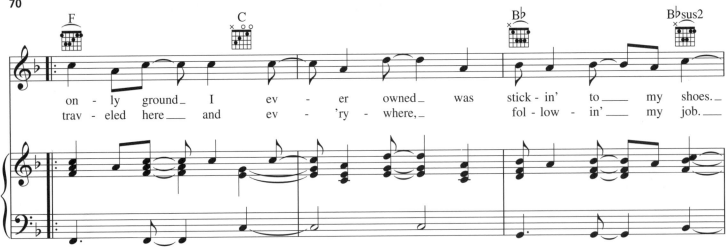

on - ly ground I ev - er owned___ was stick - in' to___ my shoes.___
trav - eled here___ and ev - 'ry - where,___ fol - low - in'___ my job.___

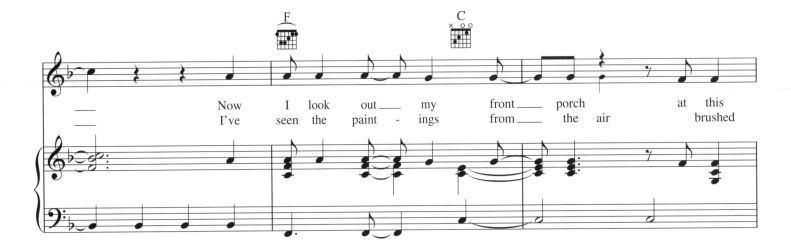

Now I look out___ my front___ porch at this
I've seen the paint - ings from___ the air brushed

pan - o - ram - ic view.___ I can sit and watch___ the fields___
by the hand___ of God.___ The moun - tains and___ the can -

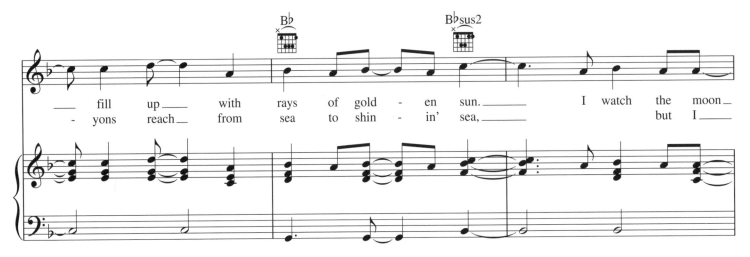

___ fill up___ with rays of gold - en sun.___ I watch the moon___
- yons reach___ from sea to shin - in' sea,___ but I___

lay on ___ the fenc - es ___ like that's where it ___ was hung. ___
can't wait ___ to get ___ back home ___ to the one He made ___ for me, ___

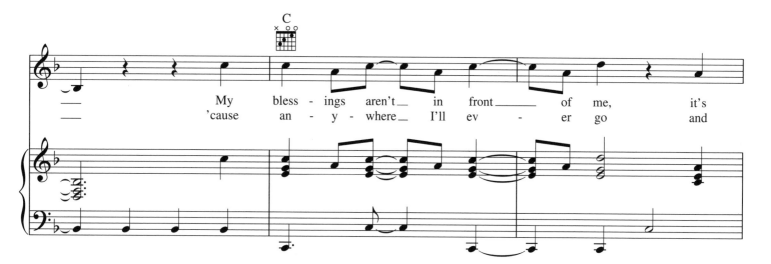

My bless - ings aren't ___ in front _____ of me, ___ it's
'cause an - y - where ___ I'll ev - er go ___ and

not a - bout ___ the land. _____ I'll nev - er beat ___ the view ___
ev - 'ry - where ___ I've been, _____ noth - in' takes my breath ___ a - way ___

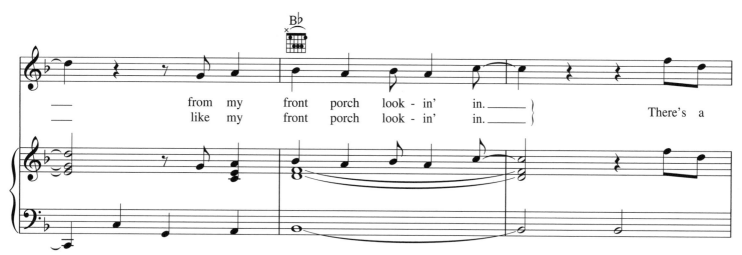

from my front porch look - in' in. _____ }
like my front porch look - in' in. _____ } There's a

car - rot top___ that can bare - ly walk with a sip - py cup___ of milk,___

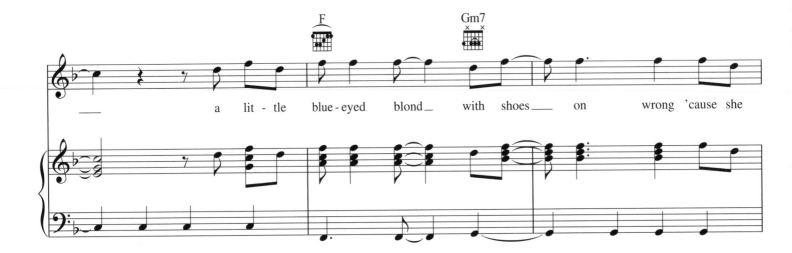

___ a lit - tle blue - eyed blond___ with shoes___ on wrong 'cause she

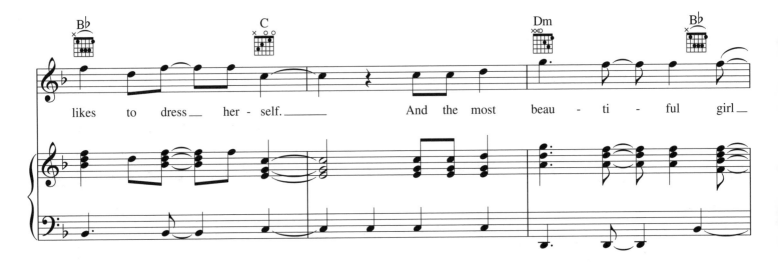

likes to dress___ her - self._____ And the most beau - ti - ful girl___

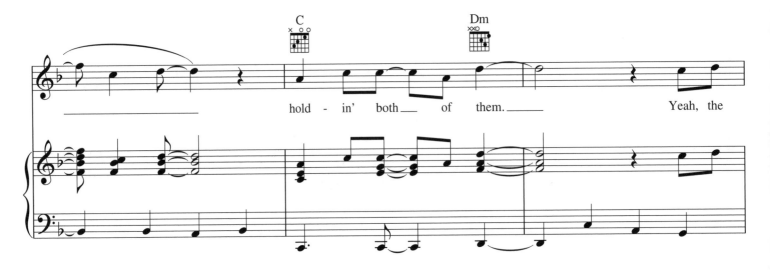

_____ hold - in' both___ of them.___ Yeah, the

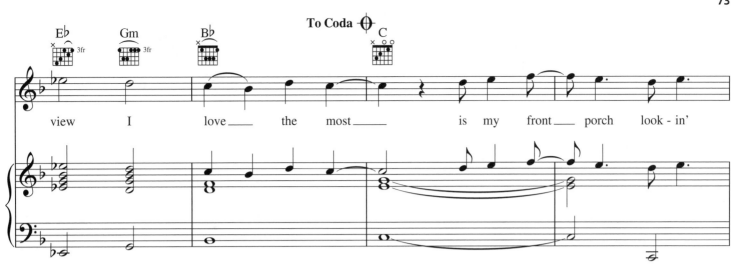

view I love___ the most___ is my front___ porch look-in'

in. _____

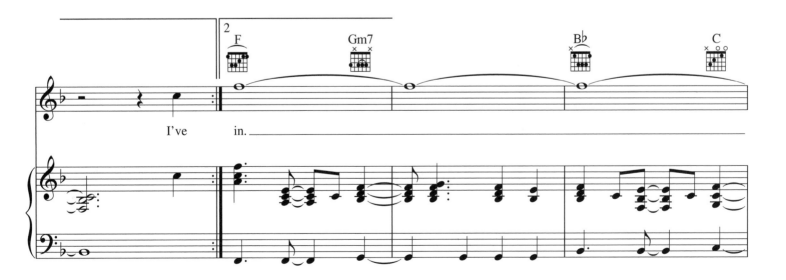

I've in. _____

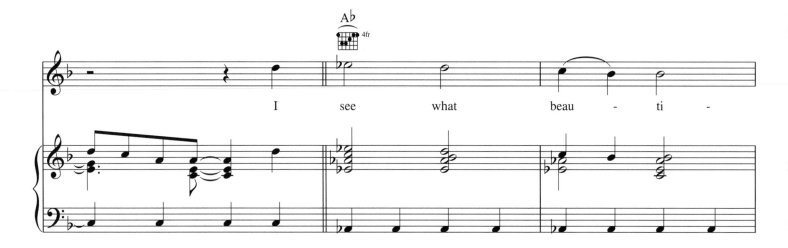

I see what beau - ti -

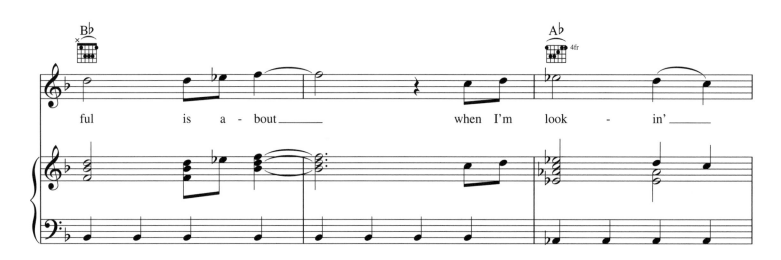

ful is a - bout_____ when I'm look - in'_____

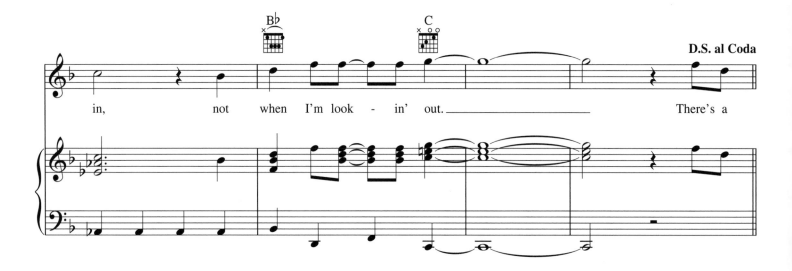

in, not when I'm look - in' out._____ There's a

D.S. al Coda

Oh, _____ the view I

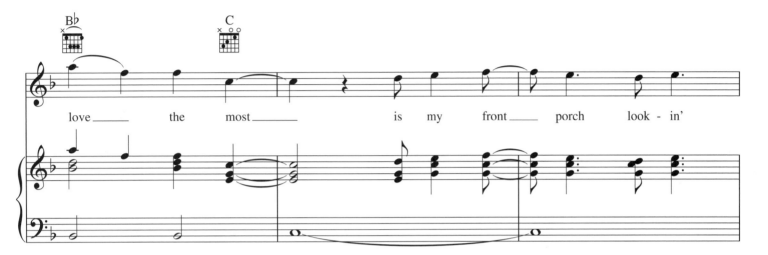

love _____ the most _____ is my front _____ porch look - in'

in. _____

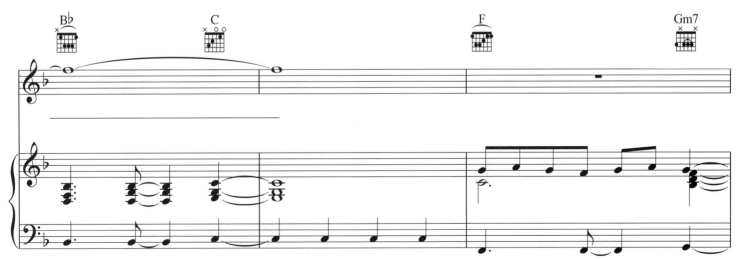

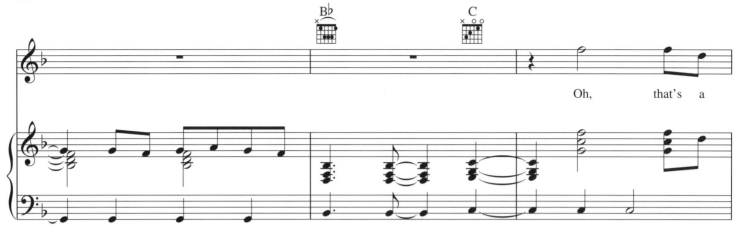

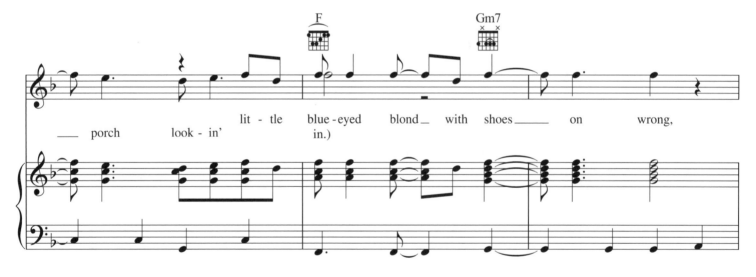

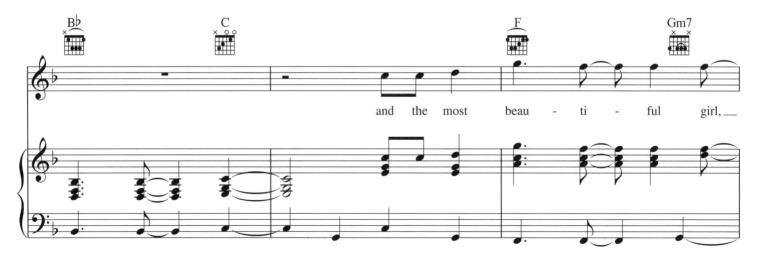

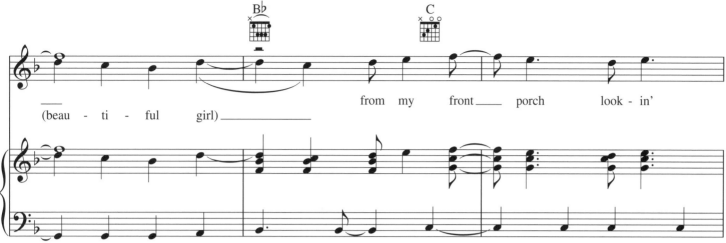

from my front____ porch look - in'

(beau - ti - ful girl)____

in.____

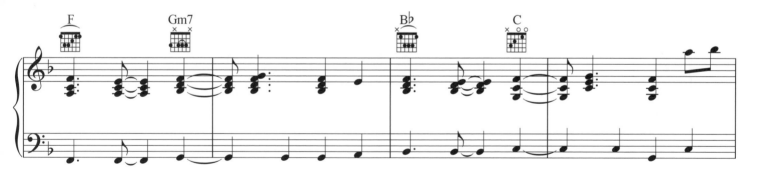

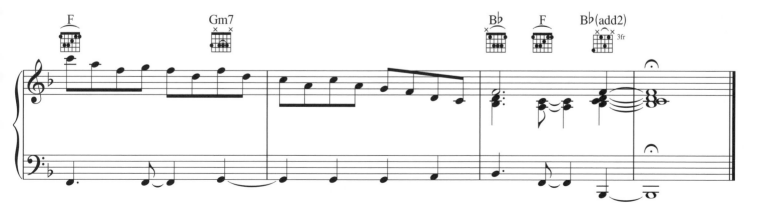

IT'S FIVE O'CLOCK SOMEWHERE

Words and Music by JIM BROWN
and DON ROLLINS

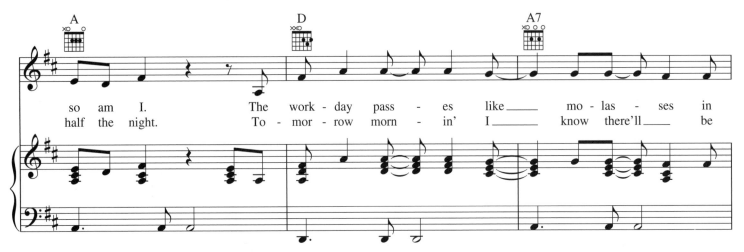

win - ter time, but it's Ju - ly. I'm get - tin' paid by the hou - r and
hell to pay, hey, but that's al - right. Ain't_ had a day off now in

old - er by the min - ute. My boss just pushed_ me o - ver the lim - it. I'd like to
o - ver a year. My Ja - mai - can va - ca - tion's gon - na start right here. If the

call him some - thin', I think I'll just call it a day.____
phone's for me, you can tell 'em I've just sailed a - way.____

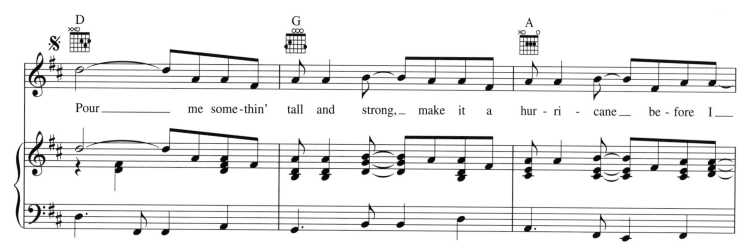

Pour____ me some - thin' tall and strong,_ make it a hur - ri - cane_ be - fore I_

go in - sane. It's on - ly half __ past twelve, __ but I don't care. __

To Coda ⊕

N.C.

It's five __ o' - clock some - where.

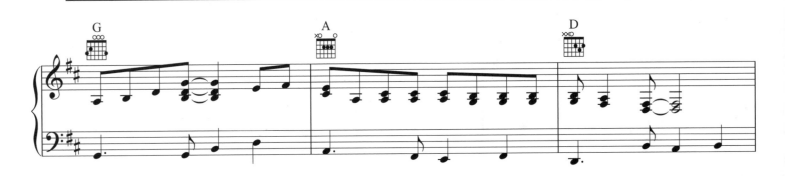

Well, It's five __ o' - clock some - where.

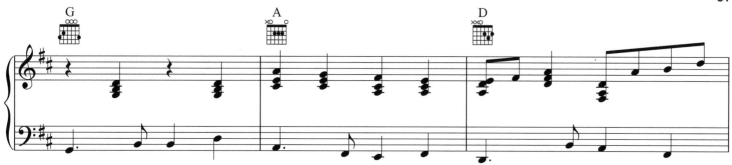

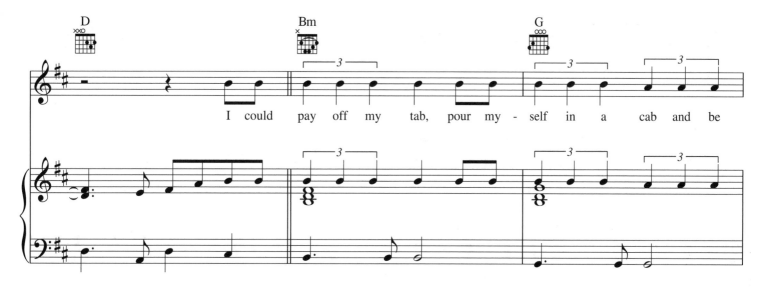

I could pay off my tab, pour my-self in a cab and be

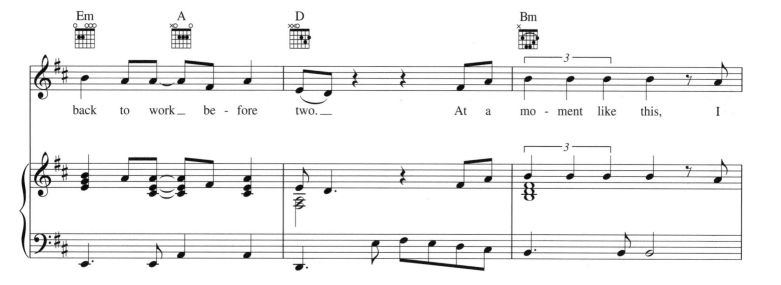

back to work_ be-fore two.__ At a mo-ment like this, I

can't help but won-der: What would Jim-my Buf-fet do?

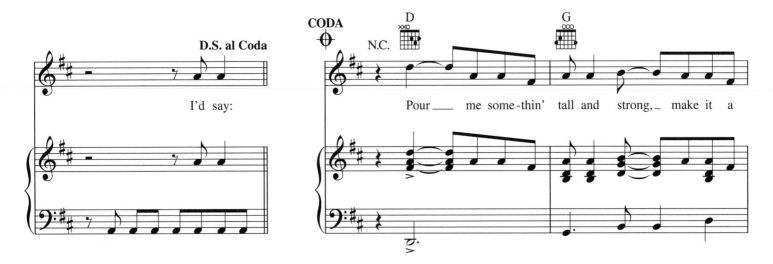

D.S. al Coda

I'd say:

CODA

N.C.

Pour ___ me some-thin' tall and strong, ___ make it a

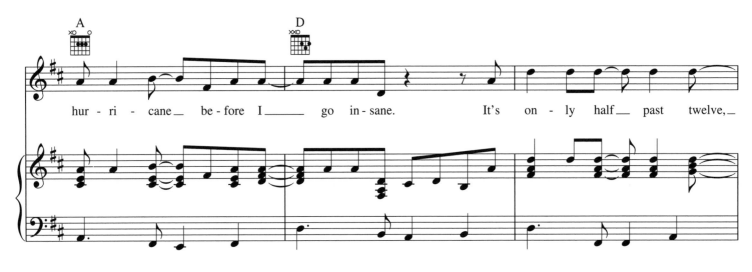

hur-ri-cane ___ be-fore I ___ go in-sane. It's on-ly half ___ past twelve, ___

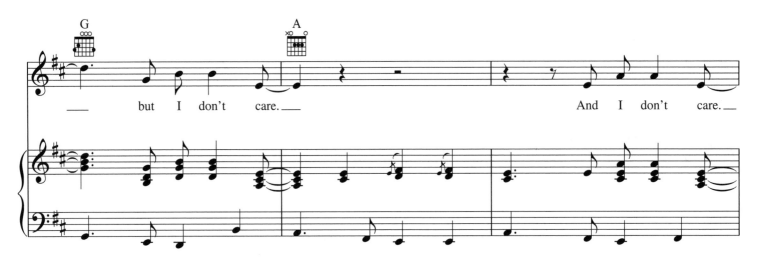

___ but I don't care. ___ And I don't care. ___

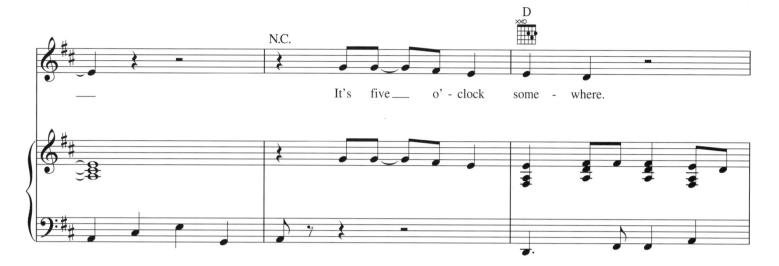

It's five___ o'- clock some - where.

Repeat and Fade

ad lib.

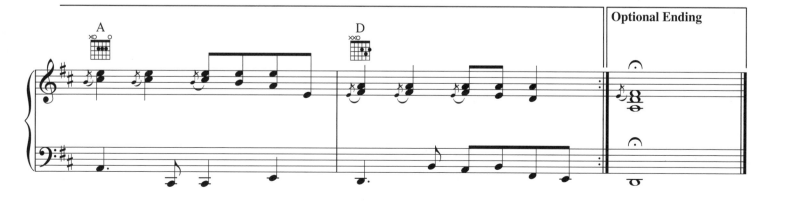

Optional Ending

RED DIRT ROAD

Words and Music by KIX BROOKS
and RONNIE DUNN

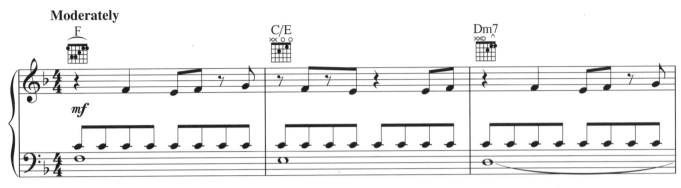

I was raised off of rural route three ___ out past ___
dad-dy did-n't like me much ___ in my

___ where the black top ends.
shack-led up G. T. O.

We'd walk to church ___ on ___ Sun-
I'd sneak ___ out ___ in the

- day morn - in', race bare - foot back ___ to John - son's fence.
mid-dle of the night, throw rocks ___ at her bed - room ___ win - dow.

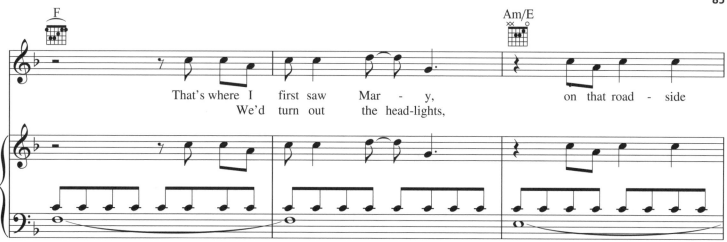

That's where I first saw Mar - y, on that road - side
We'd turn out the head-lights,

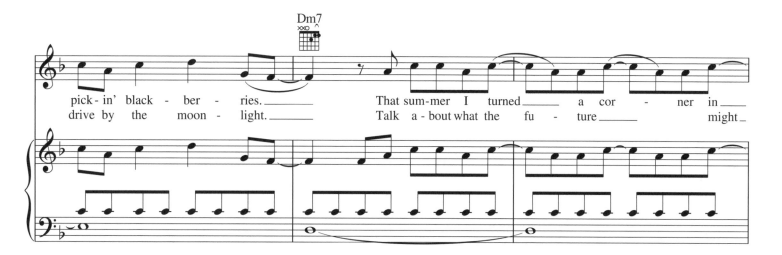

pick - in' black - ber - ries. That sum-mer I turned a cor - ner in
drive by the moon - light. Talk a - bout what the fu - ture might

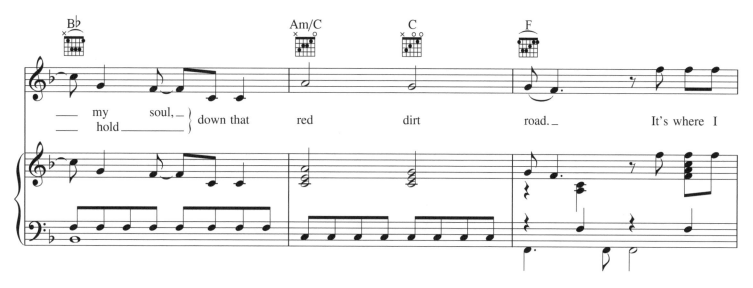

—— my soul, down that red dirt road. It's where I
—— hold down

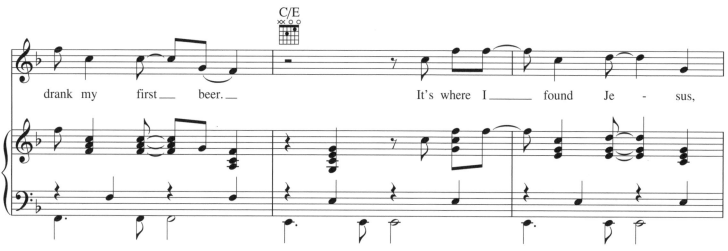

drank my first beer. It's where I found Je - sus,

where I wrecked my first car, I tore it all to piec-

-es. I learned the path to heav-en

is full of sin-ners and be-liev-ers. Learned that hap-pi-ness

on earth ain't just for high a-chiev-ers. I learned,

I've come to know ___ there's life at both ___ ends ___

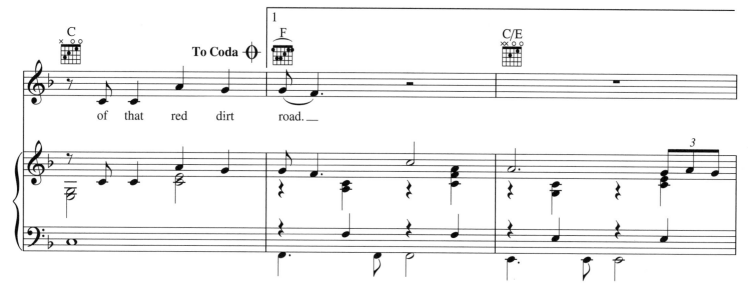

of that red dirt road. ___

Her road. ___

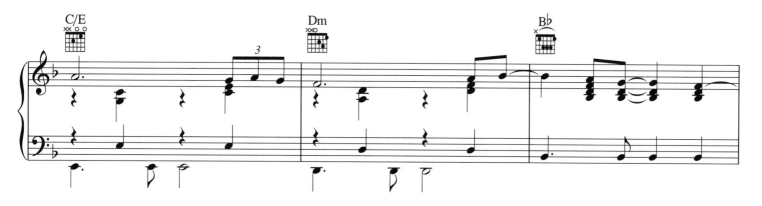

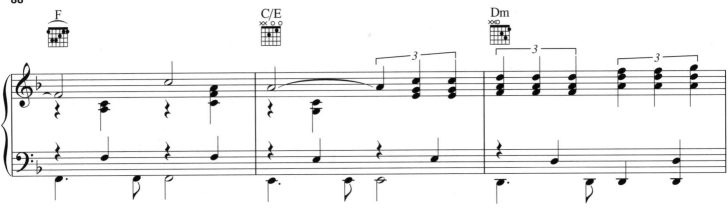

I've been out in-to__ the world__ and I came__

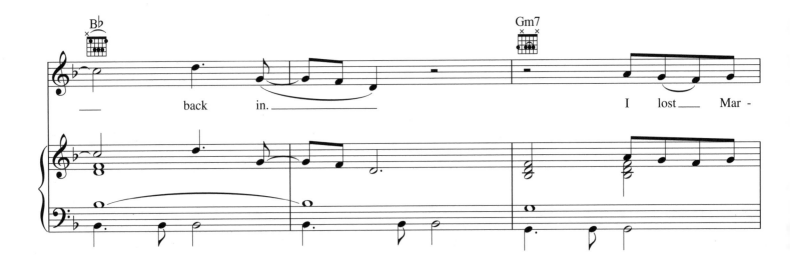

__ back in._____ I lost__ Mar -

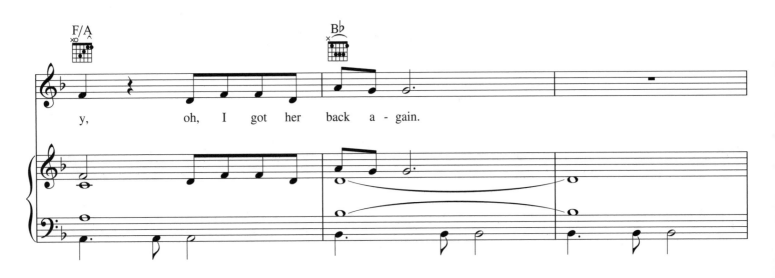

y, oh, I got her back a - gain.

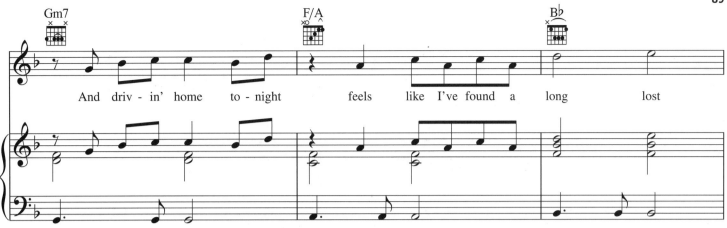

And driv- in' home to- night feels like I've found a long lost

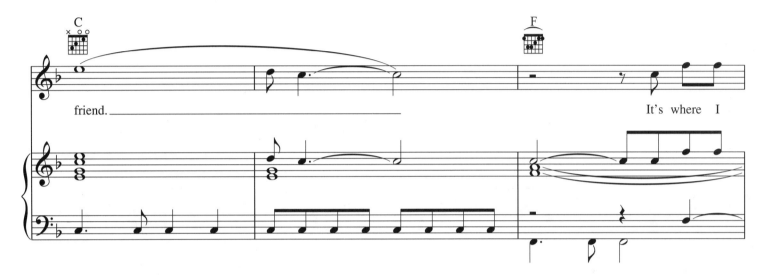

friend._____ It's where I

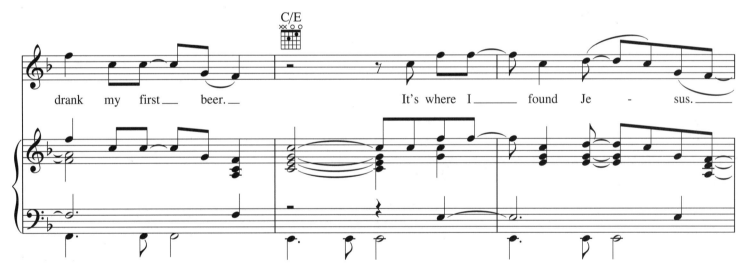

drank my first__ beer.__ It's where I_____ found Je - sus.____

Where I wrecked_ my first__ car,__ I tore it all__ to piec-

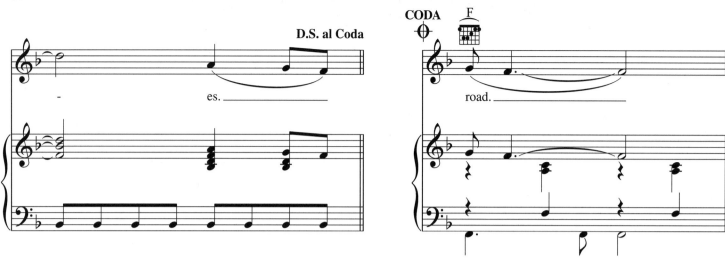

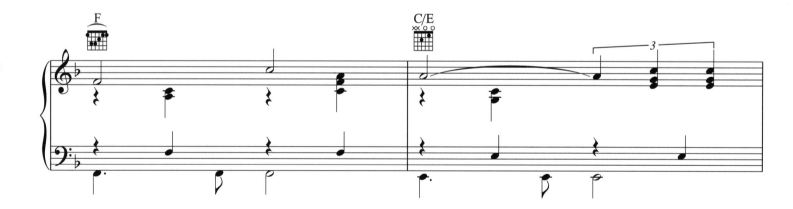

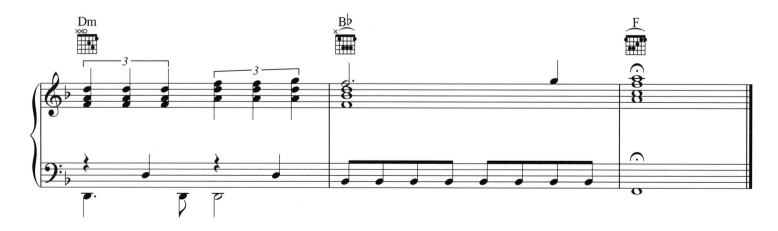

THAT'D BE ALRIGHT

Words and Music by TIM NICHOLS,
TIA SILLERS and MARK D. SANDERS

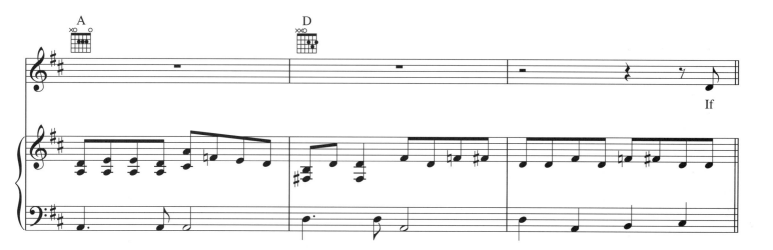

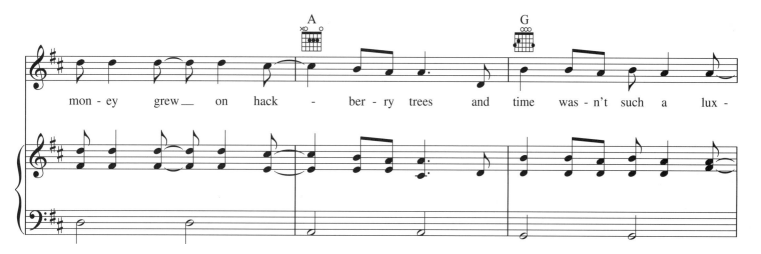

mon - ey grew __ on hack - ber - ry trees and time was - n't such a lux-

92

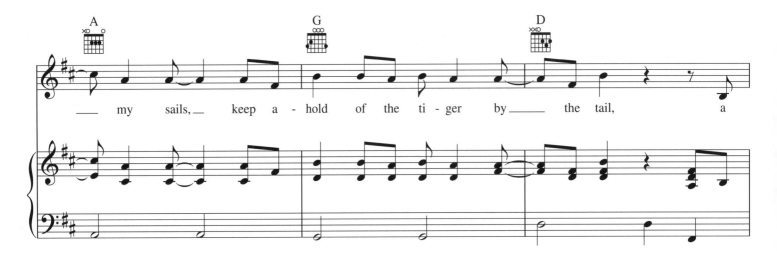

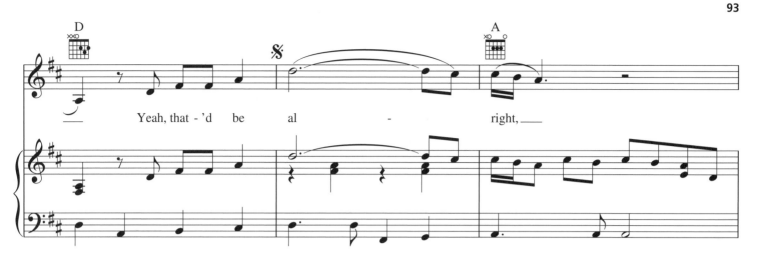

Yeah, that -'d be al - right, ___

that -'d be al '-right. If ev -'ry - bod - y ev -'ry - where_ had a

light - er load to bear_ and a lit - tle big -ger piece of the pie,___ we'd be

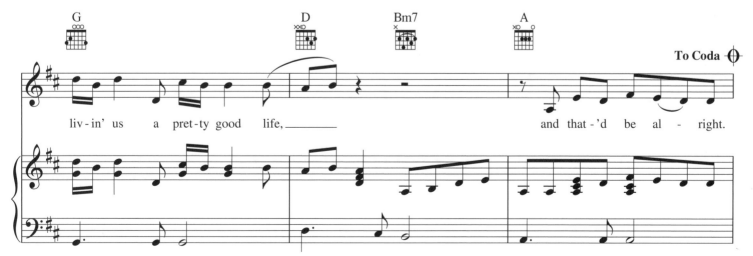

liv - in' us a pret -ty good life,_____ and that -'d be al - right.

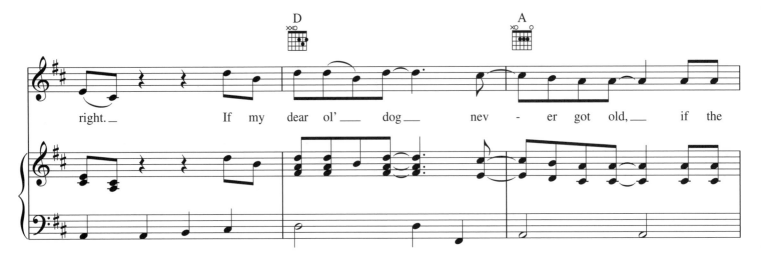

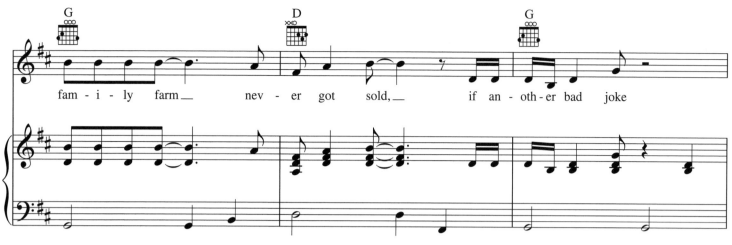

fam - i - ly farm __ nev - er got sold, __ if an - oth - er bad joke

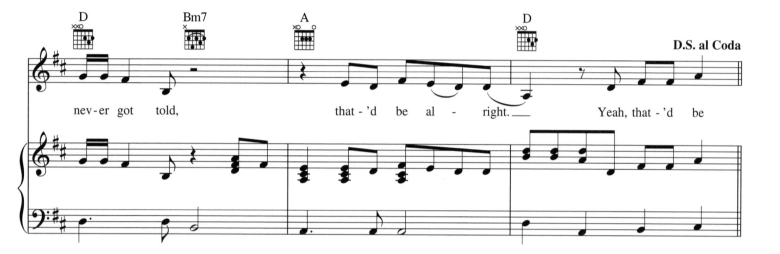

nev - er got told, that - 'd be al - right. __ Yeah, that - 'd be

Instrumental solo

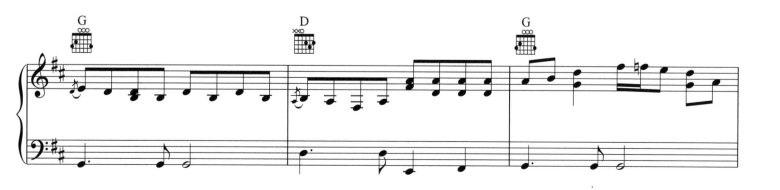

Yeah, that -'d be

Solo ends

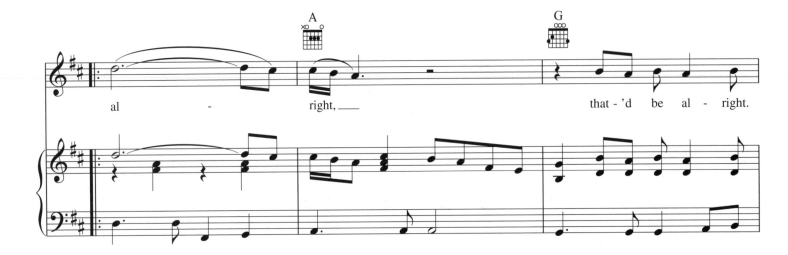

al - right, ___ that -'d be al - right.

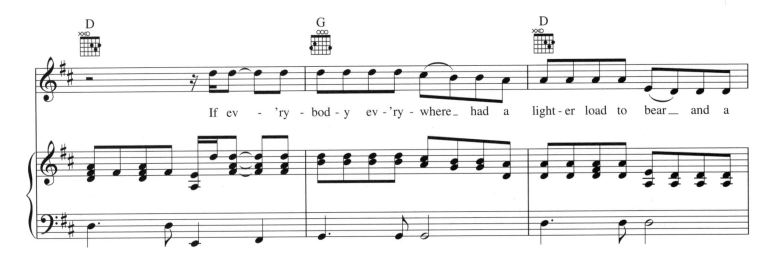

If ev - 'ry - bod - y ev -'ry - where ___ had a light - er load to bear ___ and a

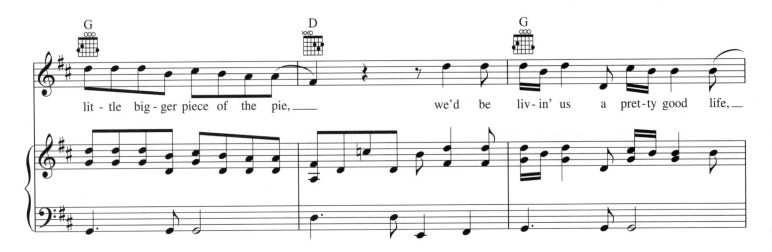

lit - tle big - ger piece of the pie, ___ we'd be liv - in' us a pret - ty good life, ___

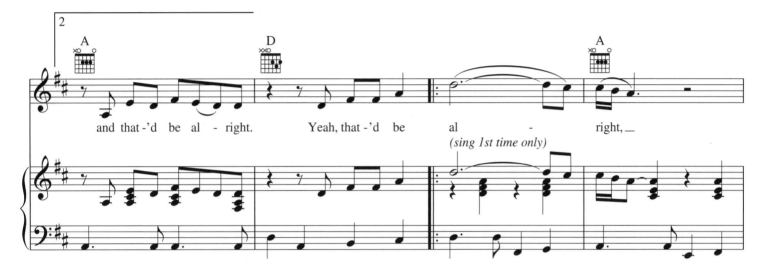

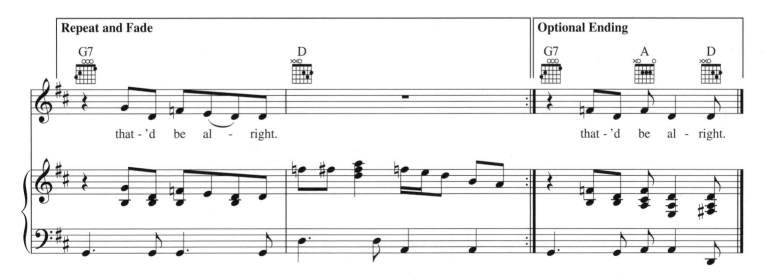

THIS ONE'S FOR THE GIRLS

Words and Music by AIMEE MAYO,
HILLARY LINDSEY and CHRIS LINDSEY

Moderately

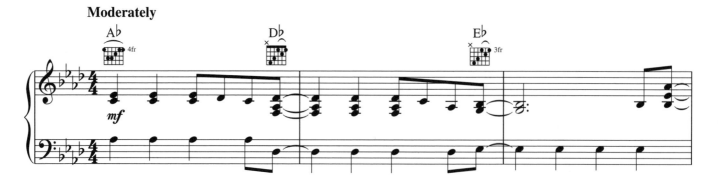

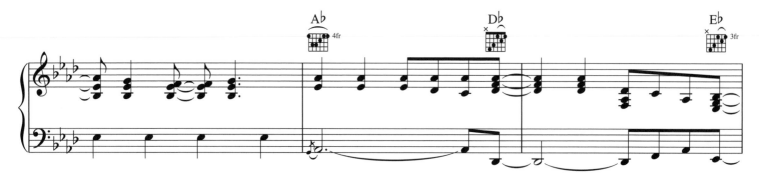

This is for all

you girls a - bout thir - teen.

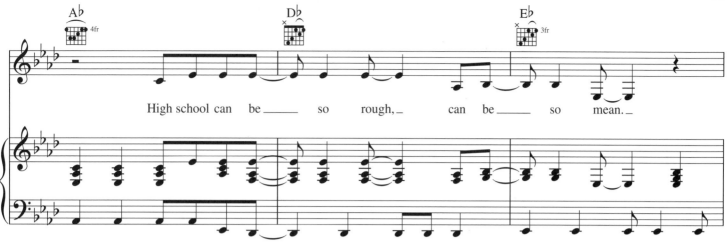

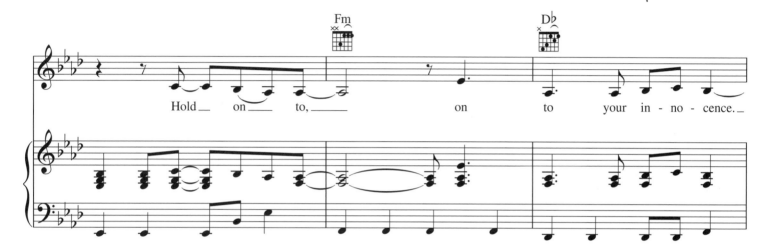

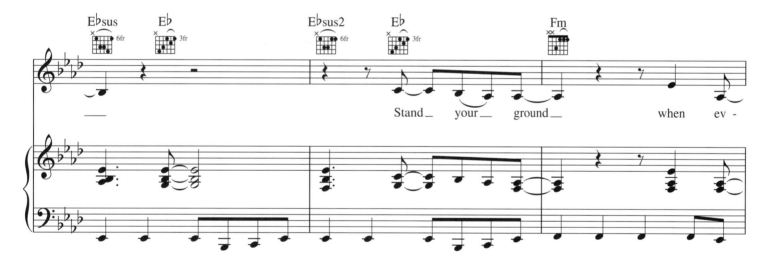

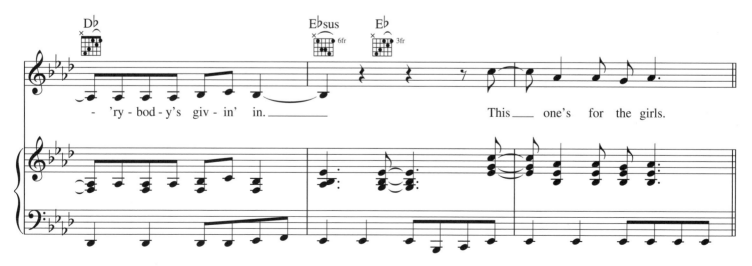

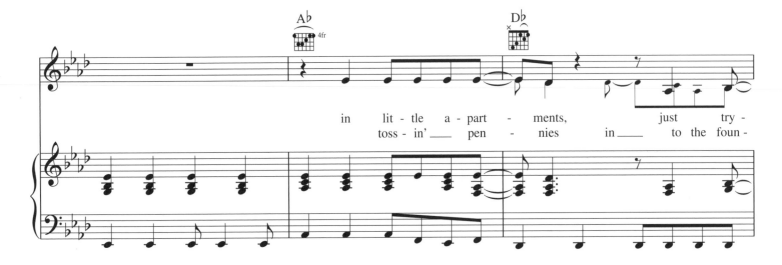

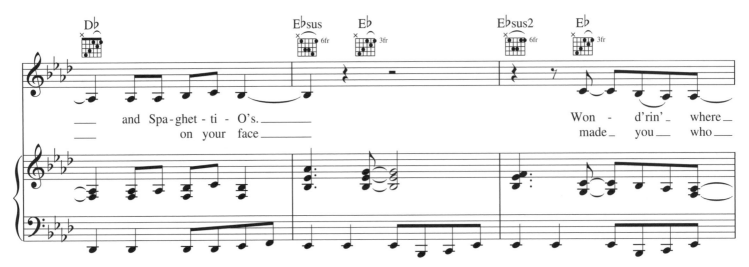

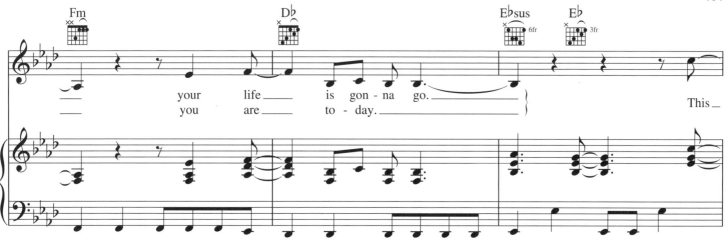

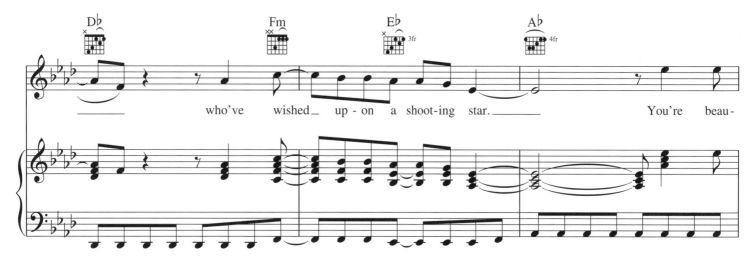

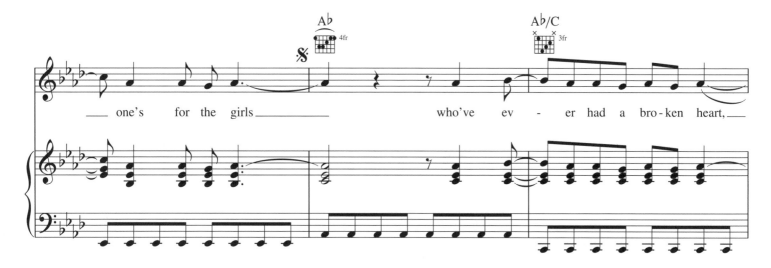

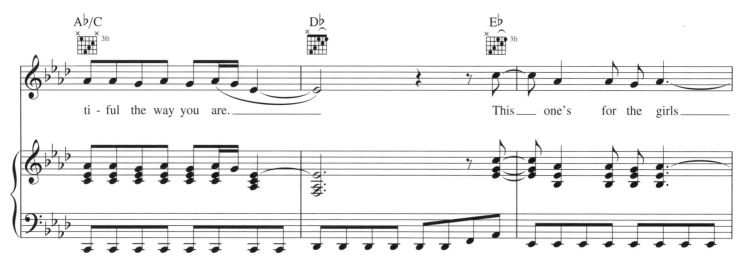

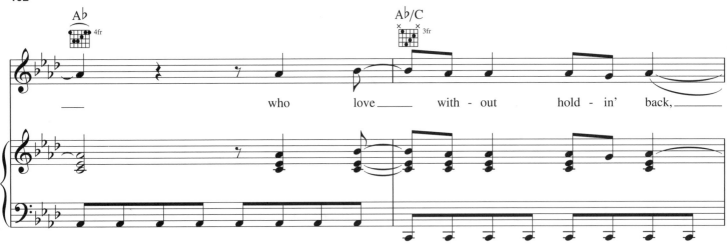

who love ____ with - out hold - in' back, ____

who dream ____ with ev - 'ry - thing they ____ have, ____

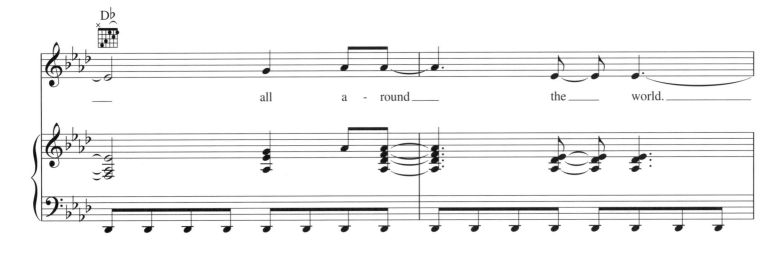

all a - round ____ the ____ world. ____

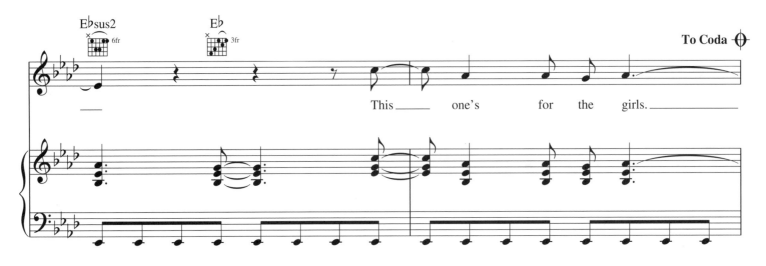

This ____ one's for the girls. ____

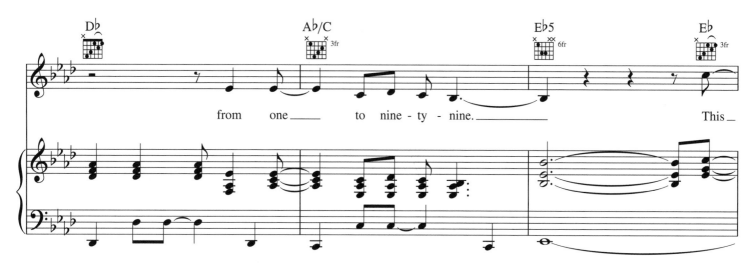

104

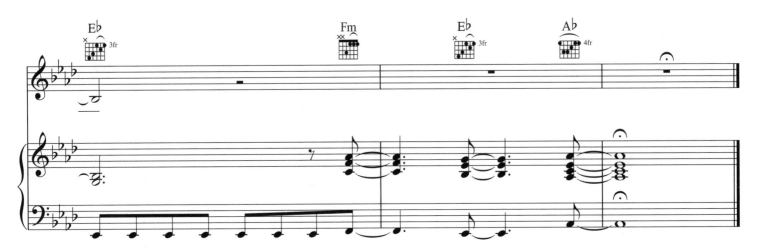

TRAVELIN' SOLDIER

Words and Music by
BRUCE ROBISON

Moderately

Two days past eight-een. He was wait-in' for the bus in his ar-my greens. Sat

down in a booth in a ca-fé there.__ Gave his or-der to a girl__ with a bow__ in her hair.__

He's a lit-tle shy so she gives him a smile. And he said, "Would you mind sit-tin' down__ for a while__ and talk-

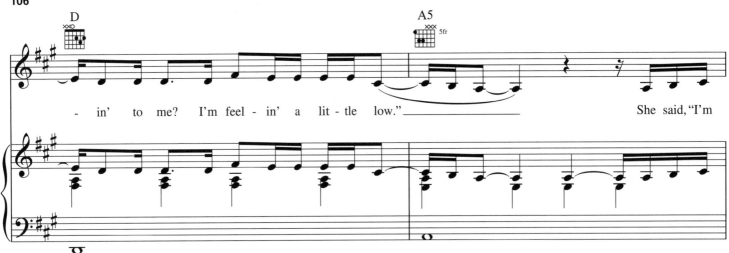

Would you mind if I___ sent__ one__ back here__ to you?"__

I _____ cried,__

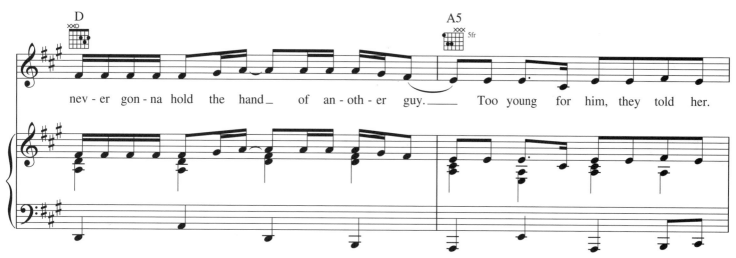

nev-er gon-na hold the hand__ of an-oth-er guy._____ Too young for him, they told her.

Wait-in' for the love of a trav-el-in' sol-dier. Our love will nev-er end.__ Wait-

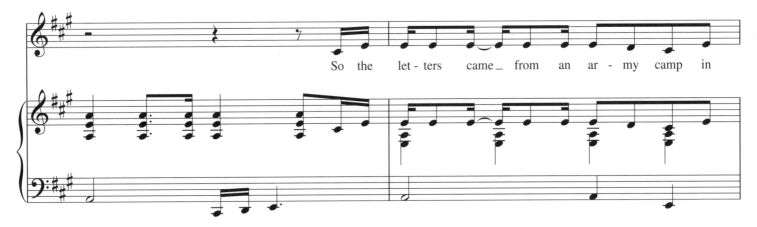

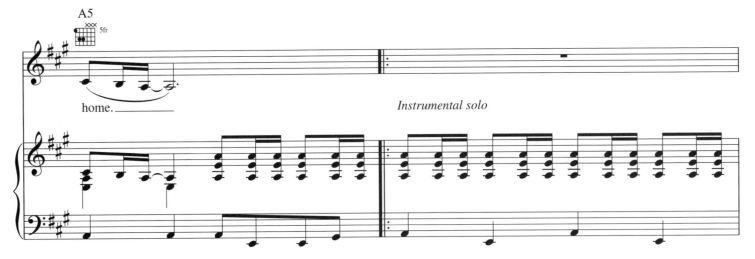

home.

Instrumental solo

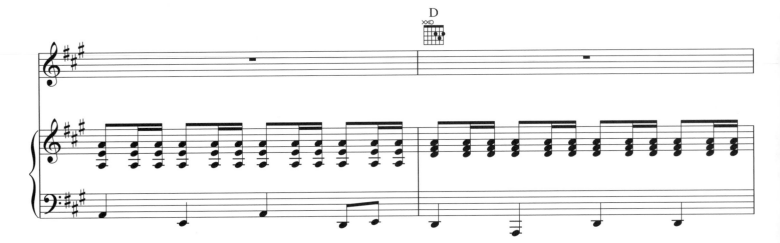

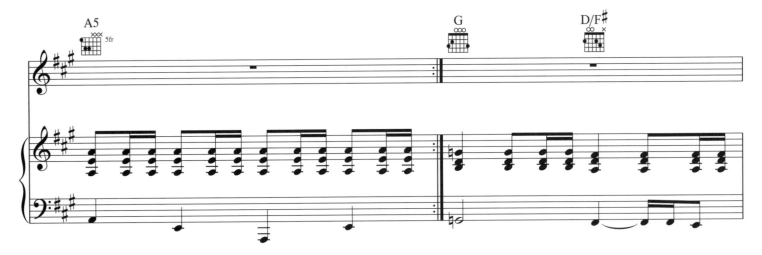

End solo

One

Fri - day night_ at a foot-ball game,_ the Lord's prayer said and the An - them sang, a man_

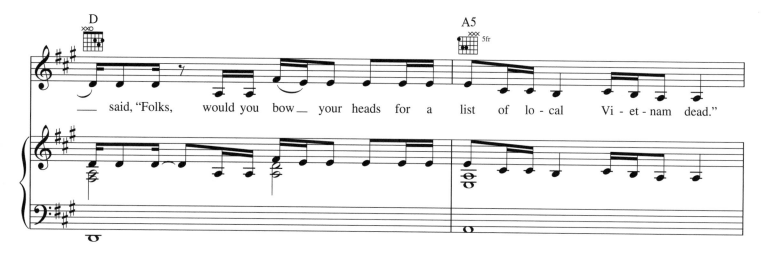

D · A5

_ said, "Folks, would you bow_ your heads for a list of lo - cal Vi - et - nam dead."

Cry - in' all a - lone un - der the stands was a

D

pic - co - lo play - er in the march - ing band. And one_ name read and no - bod - y real - ly cared_

but a pret-ty lit-tle girl __ with a bow in her __

__ hair. __ I __ cried, __

nev-er gon-na hold the hand __ of an-oth-er guy. __ Too young for him, they told her.

Wait-in' for the love of a trav-el-in' sol-dier. Our love will nev-er end. __ Wait-

-in' for the sol-dier to come back a-gain. Nev-er more to be a-lone when the

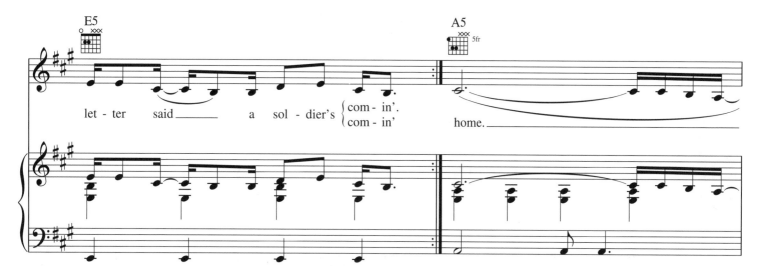

let-ter said a sol-dier's { com-in'. com-in' home.

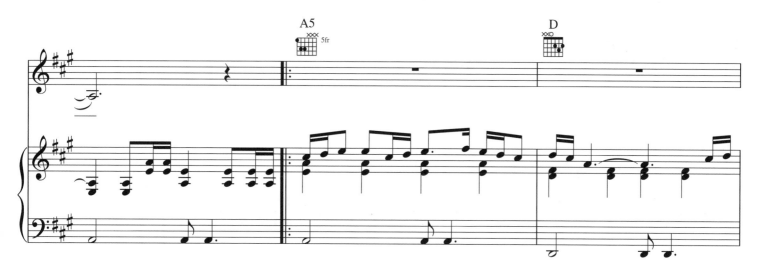

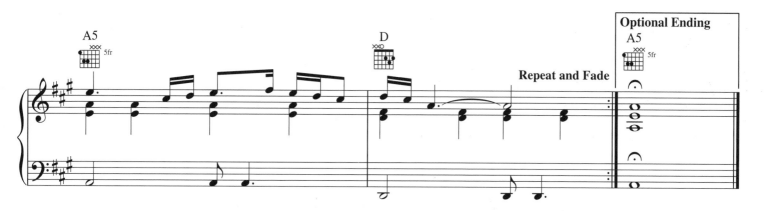

Optional Ending

Repeat and Fade

THREE WOODEN CROSSES

Words and Music by KIM WILLIAMS
and DOUG JOHNSON

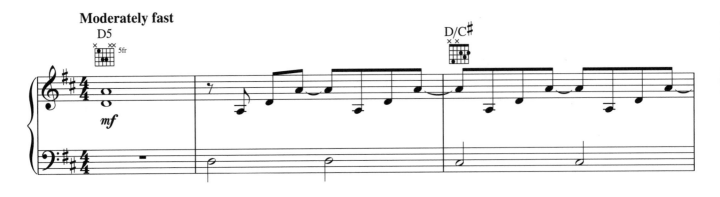

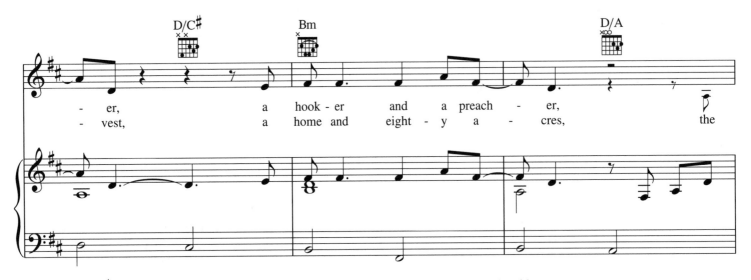

Original key: Db major. This edition has been transposed up one half-step to make it more playable.

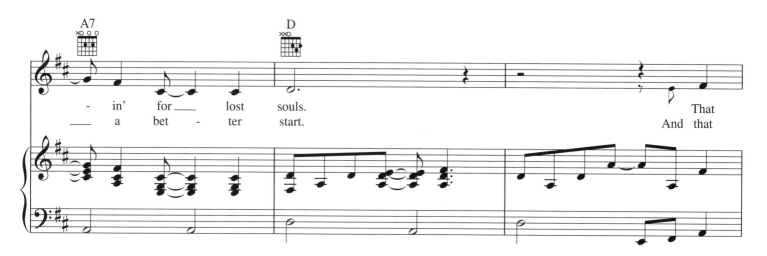

driv - er nev - er ev - er saw___ the stop___ sign
preach - er whis - pered, "Can't___ you see___ the prom - ised land?"

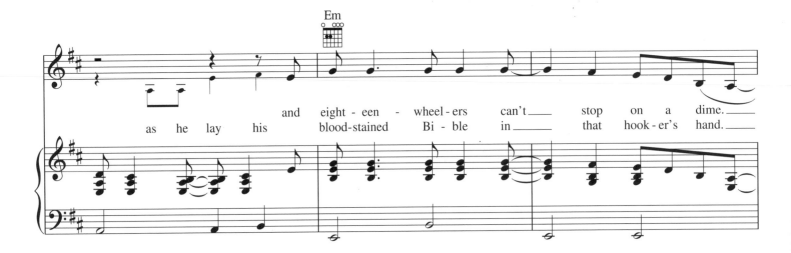

as he lay his
and eight - een - wheel - ers can't___ stop on a dime.___
blood-stained Bi - ble in___ that hook - er's hand.___

There are three wood - en cross -

- es on___ the right___ side of___ the high - way.

Why there's not four of them, ___ { heav-en on-ly knows. ___
{ (D.S.) now I guess ___ we know. ___

___ } I guess it's not what you take ___ when you leave ___

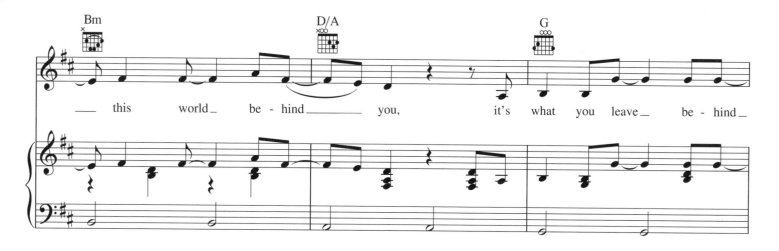

___ this world ___ be-hind ___ you, it's what you leave ___ be-hind ___

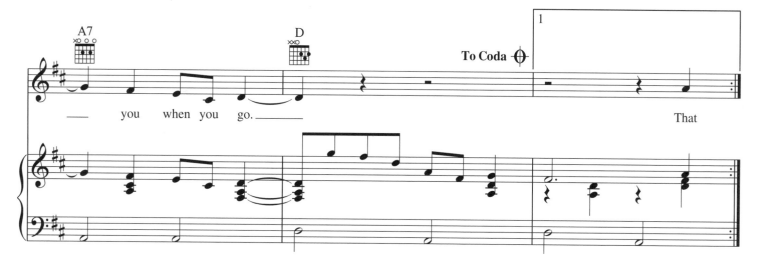

___ you when you go. ___

To Coda

That

That's a sto - ry that ___ our preach - er told ___ last

Sun - day. As he held ___ that blood - stained Bi -

- ble up for all of us ___ to see, ___ he said, "Bless the farm -

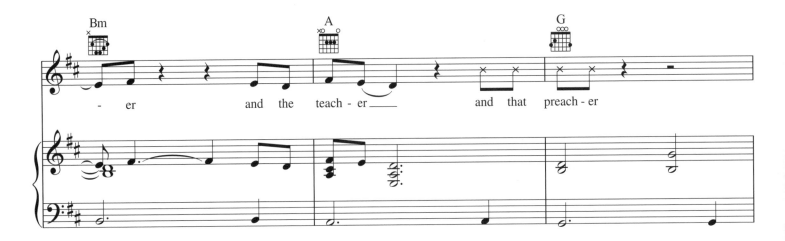

- er and the teach - er ___ and that preach - er

who gave this Bi - ble to___ my ma - ma who

read it___ to me."_____

D.S. al Coda

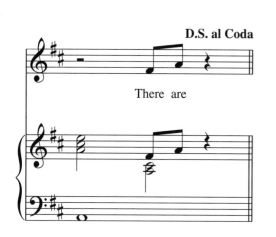

There are

CODA

There are three wood - en cross -

- es on___ the right___ side of____ the high - way.

TOUGH LITTLE BOYS

Words and Music by DONALD SAMPSON
and HARLEY ALLEN

I did-n't cry ___ when I got a black ___ eye. ___ As bad as it hurt, I just
you were to ask, ___ my ___ wife would just ___ laugh, ___ she'd say an old law ___ a - bout

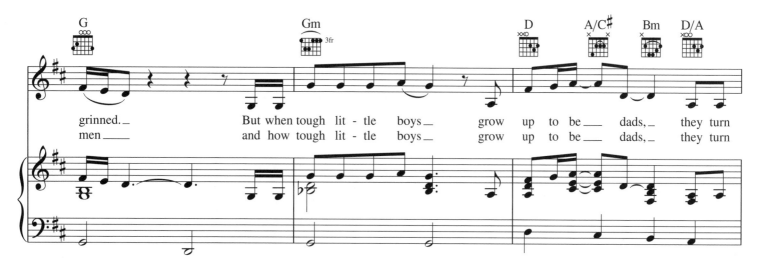

grinned. ___ But when tough lit - tle boys ___ grow up to be ___ dads, ___ they turn
men ___ and how tough lit - tle boys ___ grow up to be ___ dads, ___ they turn

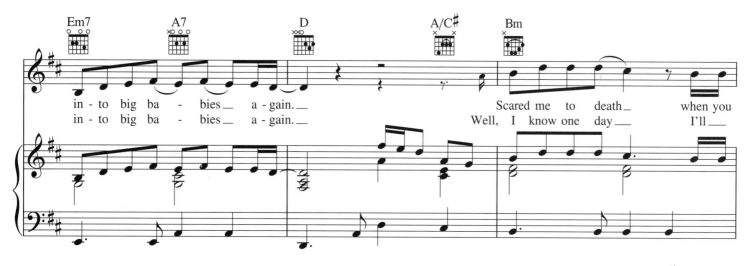

in - to big ba - bies ___ a - gain. ___ Scared me to death ___ when you
in - to big ba - bies ___ a - gain. ___ Well, I know one day ___ I'll ___

took your first steps. ___ Well, I'd fall ev - 'ry time ___ you fell down. And your
give you a - way ___ and I'm gon - na stand ___ there and smile. But

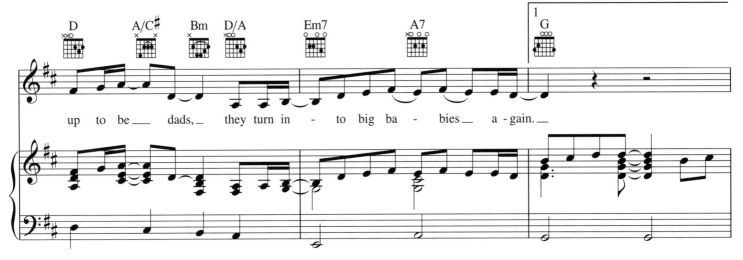

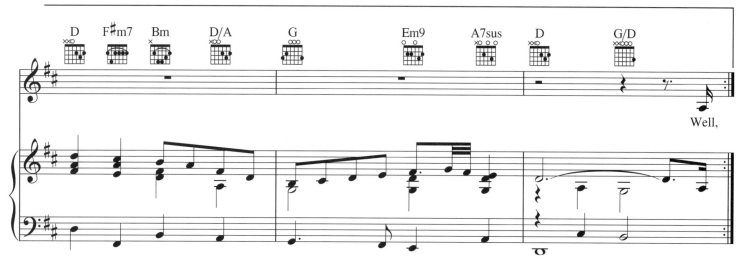

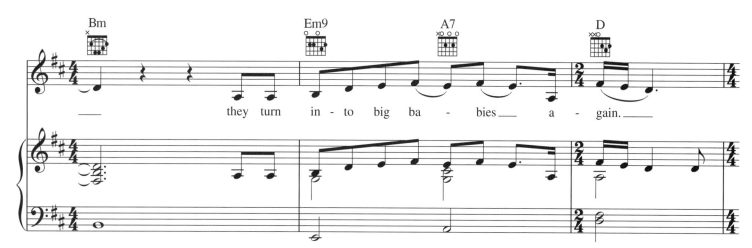

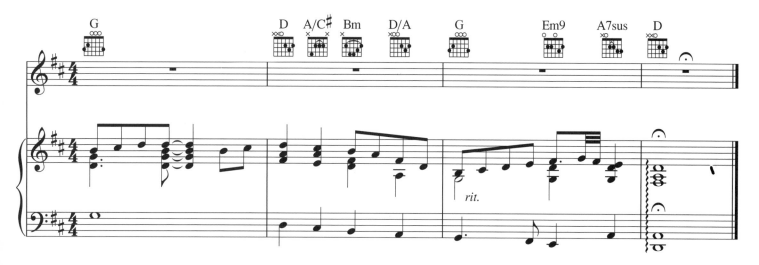

WALKING IN MEMPHIS

Words and Music by
MARC COHN

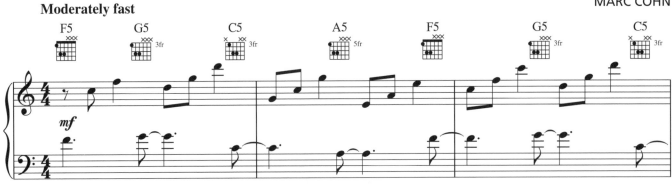

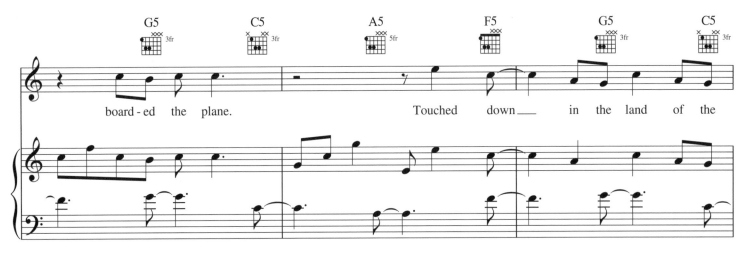

Put on ___ my blue ___ suede shoes ___ and I

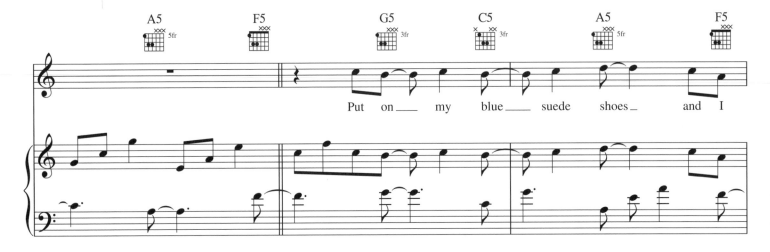

board - ed the plane.   Touched down ___ in the land of the

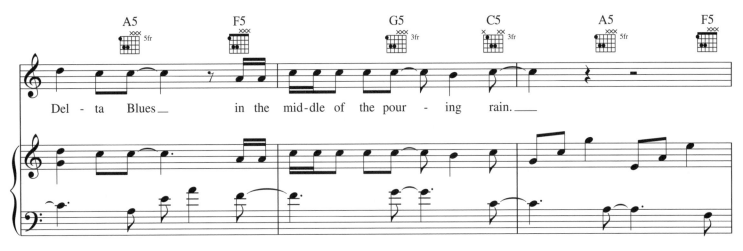

Del - ta Blues ___ in the mid - dle of the pour - ing rain. ___

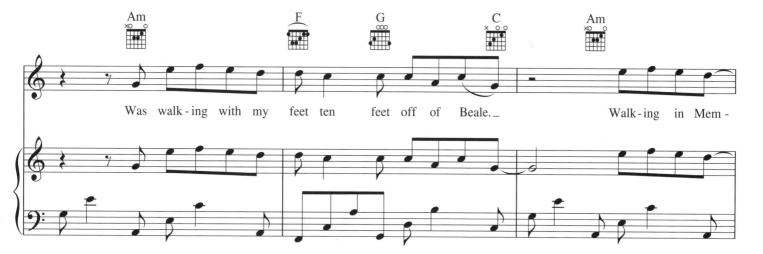

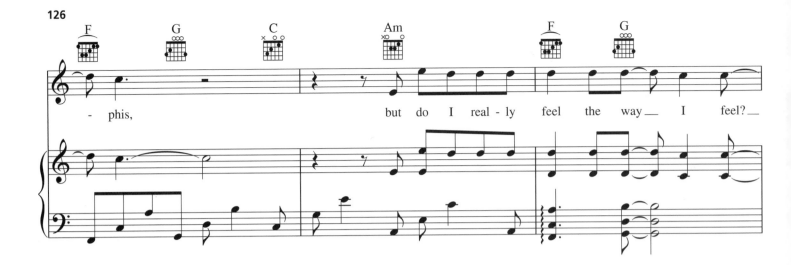

-phis, but do I real-ly feel the way ___ I feel? ___

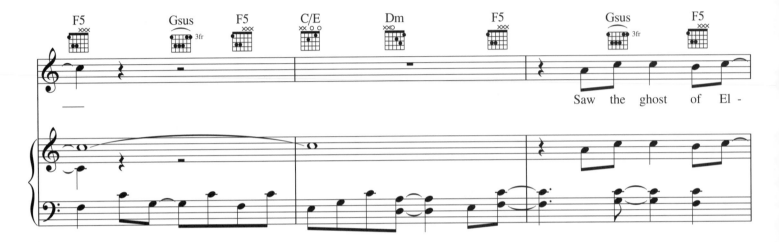

___ Saw the ghost of El-

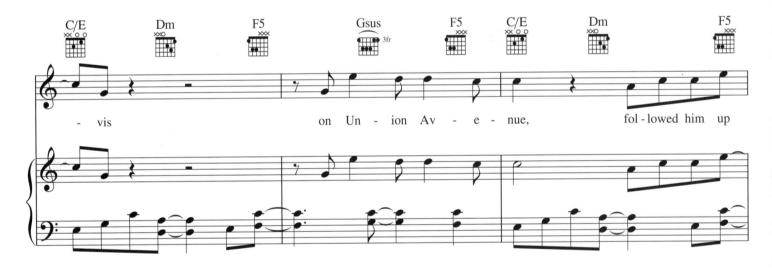

-vis on Un-ion Av - e - nue, fol-lowed him up

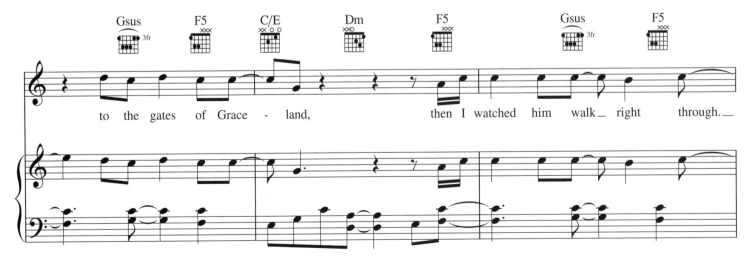

to the gates of Grace-land, then I watched him walk ___ right through. ___

Now se - cur - i - ty, they did not_ see him; they just

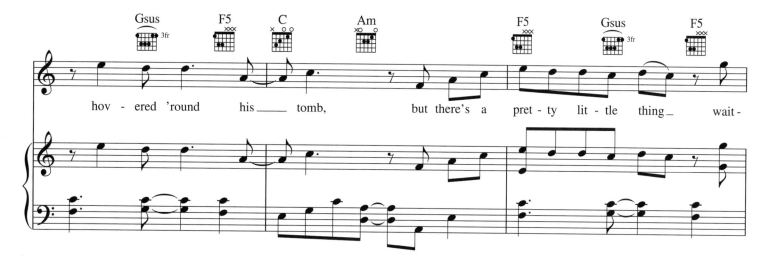

hov - ered 'round his _ tomb, but there's a pret - ty lit - tle thing _ wait-

ing for the King _ down in the Jun - gle Room. When I was walk - ing in Mem-

- phis I was walk - ing with my feet ten feet off of Beale. _

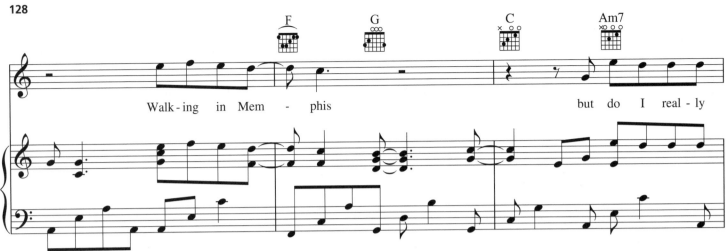

Walk - ing in Mem - phis but do I real - ly

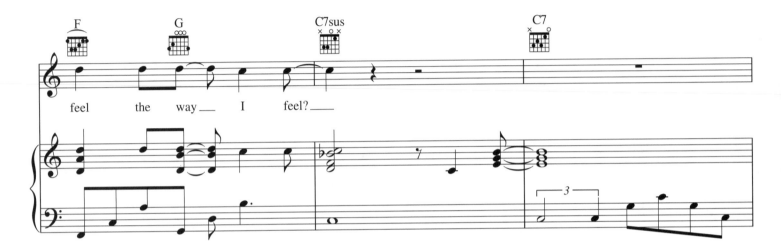

feel the way__ I feel?__

They've__ got cat - fish on the ta -

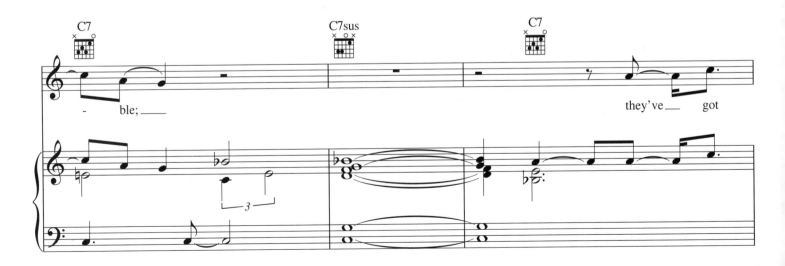

- ble;__ they've__ got

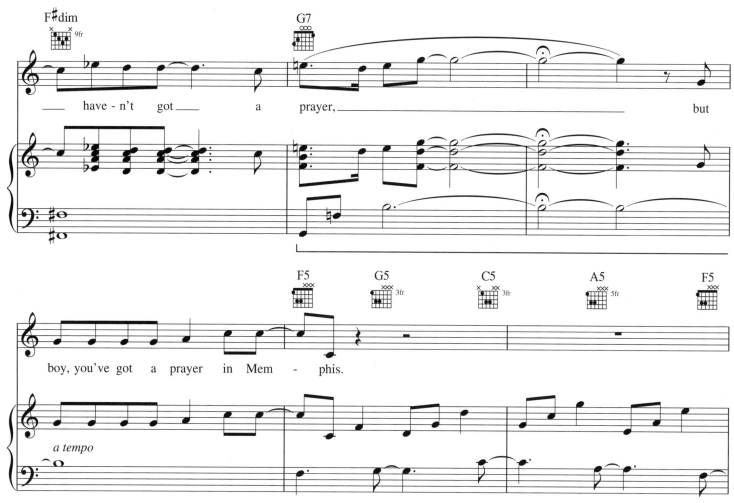

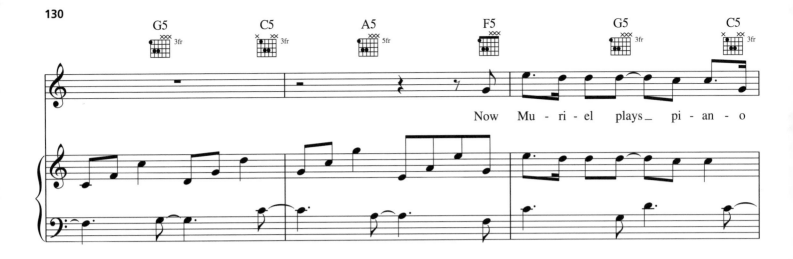

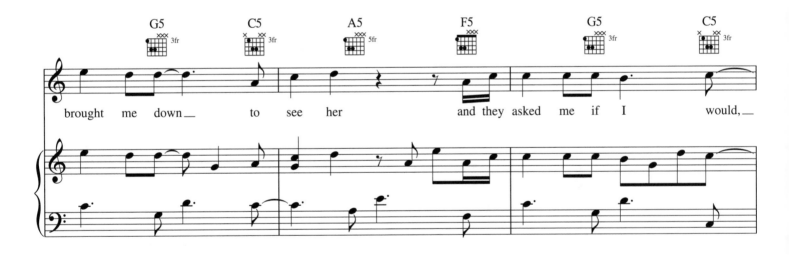

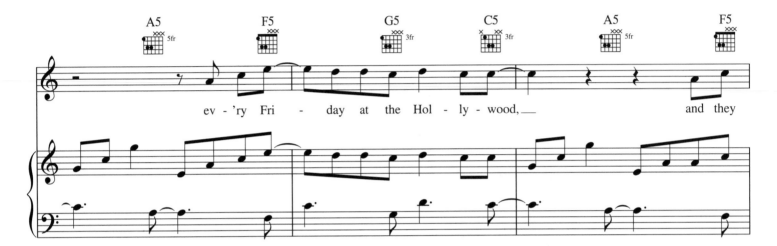

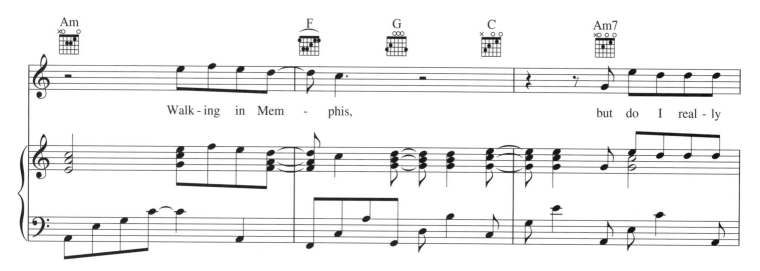

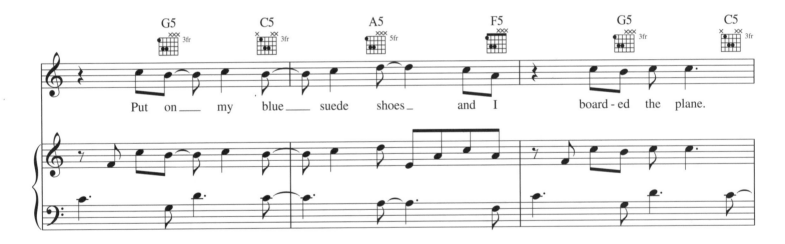

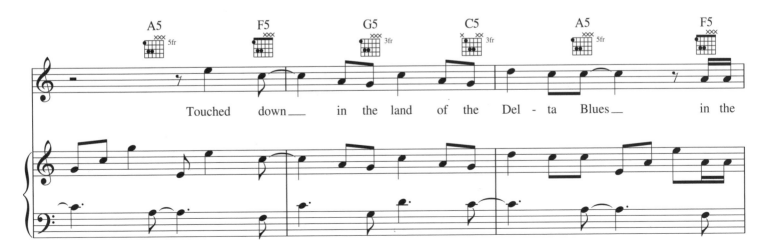

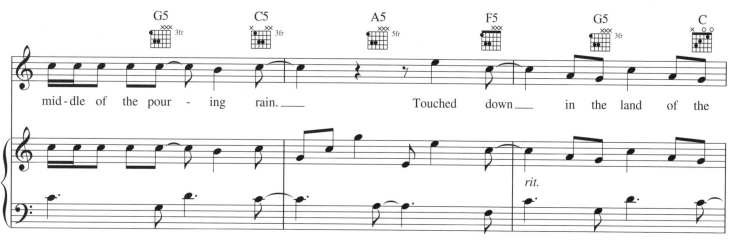

mid - dle of the pour - ing rain. ___ Touched down ___ in the land of the

Del - ta Blues ___ in the mid - dle of the pour - ing rain.

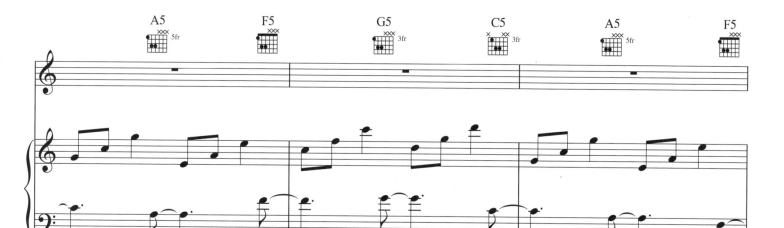

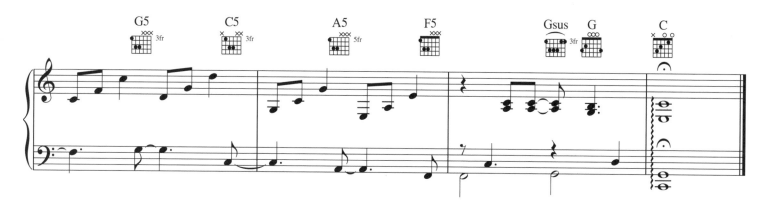

WAVE ON WAVE

Words and Music by PAT GREEN,
DAVID NEUHAUSER and JUSTIN POLLARD

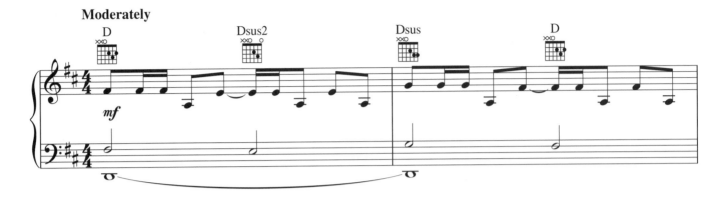

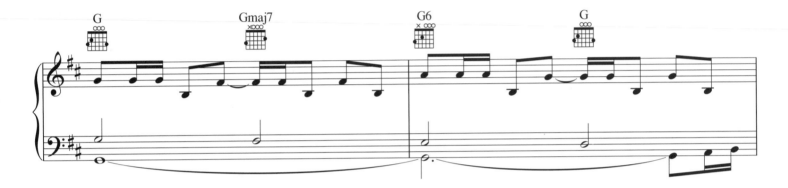

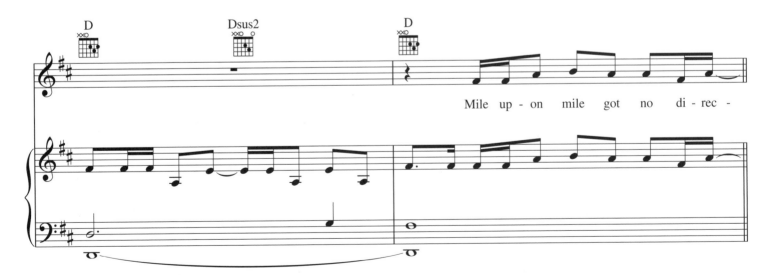

Mile up-on mile got no di-rec-

what we're seek - in' is ___ the truth.
Not a - fraid ___ an - y - more. ___

I'm not look - in' for a hap - py end - ing.
She said, "You know I al - ways had you, ba - by,

All I'm look - in' for ___ is you. ___
just wait - in' for you to find ___ what you ___ were look - in' for." ___

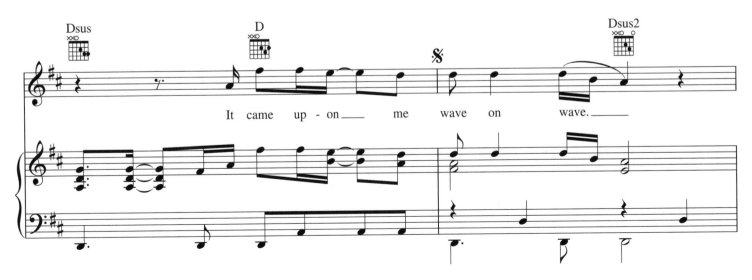

It came up - on ___ me wave on wave. ___

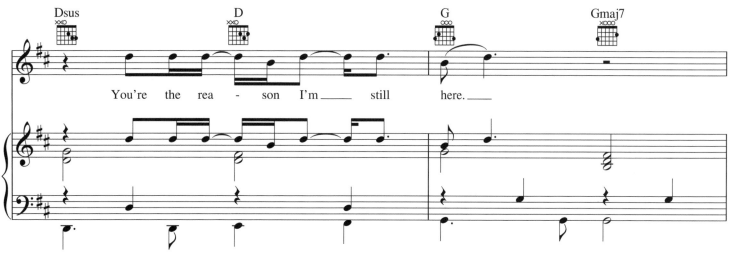

wave, _____

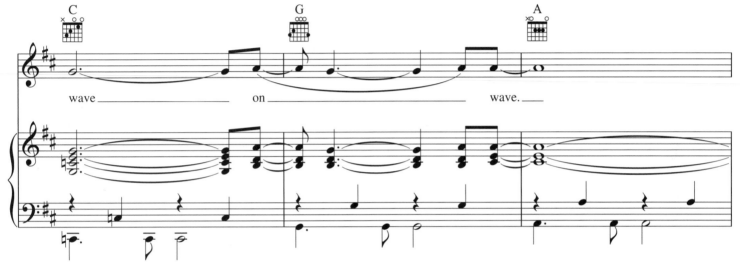

wave _____ on _____ wave. _____

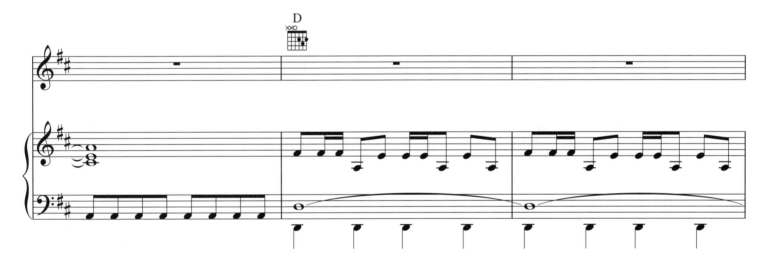

D.S. al Coda

And it came up - on ___ me

CODA

The clouds broke and the an - gels cried, _____

"You ain't got - ta walk _____ a - lone. _____

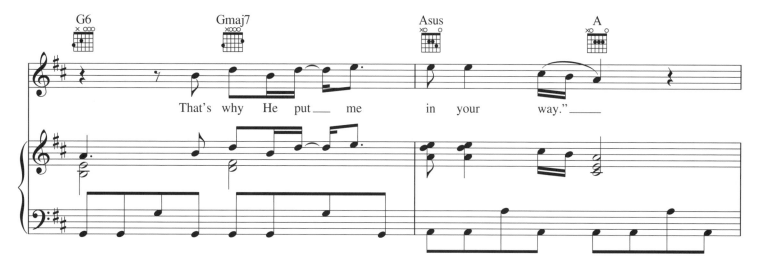

That's why He put _____ me in your way." _____

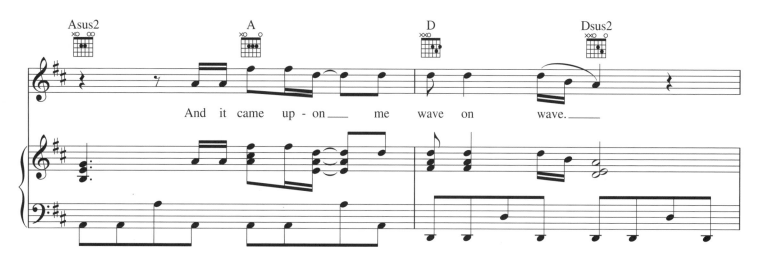

And it came up - on _____ me wave on wave. _____

Yeah, it came up-on___ me wave on wave.

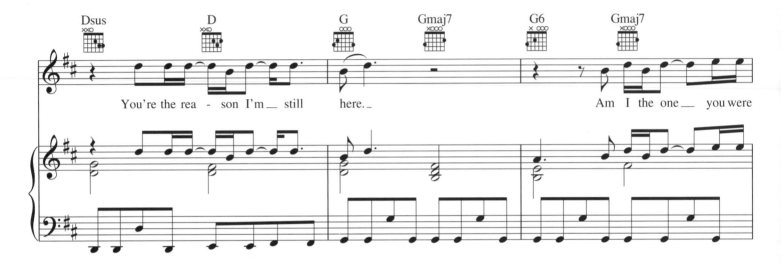

You're the rea - son I'm___ still here.___ Am I the one___ you were

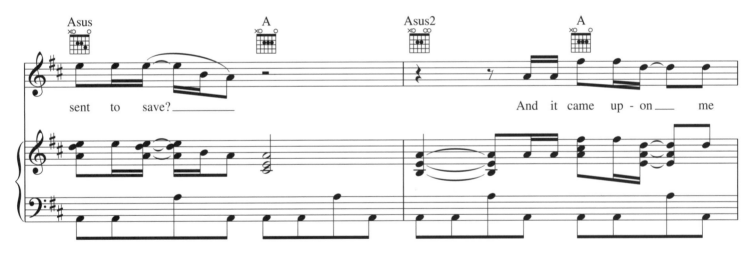

sent to save?___ And it came up-on___ me

Repeat and Fade · **Optional Ending**

wave on wave.___ Yeah, it came up-on___ me wave on wave.

Contemporary & Classic Country

More great country hits from Hal Leonard arranged for piano and voice with guitar chords.

#1 Country Hits of the Nineties – 2nd Edition
The second edition of this great compilation includes 26 hits: Achy Breaky Heart • Boot Scootin' Boogie • Chattahoochee • Check Yes or No • Friend in Low Places • Longneck Bottle • Love Without End, Amen • My Maria • She Is His Only Need • Wide Open Spaces • You're Still the One • more.
00311699..$12.95

51 Country Standards
A collection of 51 of country's biggest hits, including: (Hey Won't You Play) Another Somebody Done Somebody Wrong Song • By the Time I Get to Phoenix • Could I Have This Dance • Daddy Sang Bass • Forever and Ever, Amen • God Bless the U.S.A. • Green Green Grass of Home • Islands in the Stream • King of the Road • Little Green Apples • Lucille • Mammas Don't Let Your Babies Grow Up to Be Cowboys • Ruby Don't Take Your Love to Town • Stand by Me • Through the Years • Your Cheatin' Heart.
00359517..$14.95

100 Most Wanted
Highlights: A Boy Named Sue • Break It to Me Gently • Crying My Heart out over You • Heartbroke • I.O.U. • I Know a Heartache When I See One • Mammas Don't Let Your Babies Grow Up to Be Cowboys • My Heroes Have Always Been Cowboys • Stand by Me • Save the Last Dance for Me • You're the First Time I've Thought About Leaving • You're the Reason God Made Oklahoma • many more.
00360730..$15.95

Hot Country Dancin'
Over 30 toe-tapping, boot-scootin' favorites guaranteed to get you dancing! Includes: Achy Breaky Heart • Friends in Low Places • Here's a Quarter (Call Someone Who Cares) • Hey, Good Lookin' • I Feel Lucky • and more.
00311621................$12.95

The Award-Winning Songs of the Country Music Association – 1984-1996
40 country award-winners, including: Achy Breaky Heart • Ain't That Lonely Yet • Baby's Got Her Blue Jeans On • Boot Scootin' Boogie • Daddy's Hands • Down at the Twist and Shout • Forever and Ever, Amen • Friends in Low Places • God Bless the U.S.A. • I Swear • The Keeper of the Stars • Where've You Been • and more. Also includes a photo library of the winners.
00313081..$17.95

Contemporary Country
Features 49 hot country hits: Amazed • Blue • A Broken Wing • Cowboy Take Me Away • He Didn't Have to Be • I Love You • I'm Alright • Little Red Rodeo • Longneck Bottle • Ready to Run • Single White Female • many more!
00310587..$17.95

Country Love
27 songs of down-home lovin': The Battle Hymn of Love • Check Yes or No • Could I Have This Dance • Grow Old With Me • The Keeper of the Stars • Let's Go to Vegas • More Than You'll Ever Know • She Is His Only Need • You Decorated My Life • You're Still the One • and more.
00310516..$14.95

20th Century Country Music
Over 70 country classics representative of a century's worth of music, including: All the Gold in California • Always on My Mind • Amazed • Blue Moon of Kentucky • Boot Scootin' Boogie • Breathe • Crazy • Friends in Low Places • Harper Valley P.T.A. • Hey, Good Lookin' • Ring of Fire • and more.
00310673..$19.95

Country Inspiration – 2nd Edition
23 sentimental favorites, including: Brotherly Love • I Saw the Light • Love Can Build a Bridge • Love Without End, Amen • The Vows Go Unbroken • Why Me Lord? • and more.
00311616................$10.95

Good Ol' Country
58 old-time favorites: Candy Kisses • Cold, Cold Heart • Crazy • Crying in the Chapel • Deep in the Heart of Texas • Faded Love • Green Green Grass of Home • Hey, Good Lookin' • I Can't Stop Loving You • Sweet Dreams • Tennessee Waltz • You Are My Sunshine • You Don't Know Me • more.
00310517..$14.95

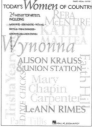

The Best Contemporary Country Ballads
30 heart-felt hits, including: After All This Time • Alibis • The Greatest Man I Never Knew • I Can Love You like That • I Meant Every Word He Said • I Want to Be Loved like That • If Tomorrow Never Comes • One Boy, One Girl • When You Say Nothing at All • Where've You Been • more.
00310116..$14.95

Today's Women of Country
Includes 24 hits by top artists such as LeAnn Rimes, Reba McEntire, Faith Hill, Pam Tillis, Trisha Yearwood and others. Songs include: Blue • Down at the Twist and Shout • The Greatest Man I Never Knew • I Feel Lucky • Mi Vida Loca (My Crazy Life) • When You Say Nothing at All • more!
00310446..$12.95

FOR MORE INFORMATION, SEE YOUR LOCAL MUSIC DEALER, OR WRITE TO:

HAL•LEONARD® CORPORATION

7777 W. BLUEMOUND RD. P.O. BOX 13819 MILWAUKEE, WI 53213
www.halleonard.com

Prices, contents, and availability subject to change without notice.

0201

COUNTRY MUSIC HALL OF FAME

SONGBOOK SERIES

The Country Music Hall of Fame was founded in 1961 by the Country Music Association (CMA). Each year, new members are elected – and these books are the first to represent all of its members with photos, biographies and music selections related to each individual.

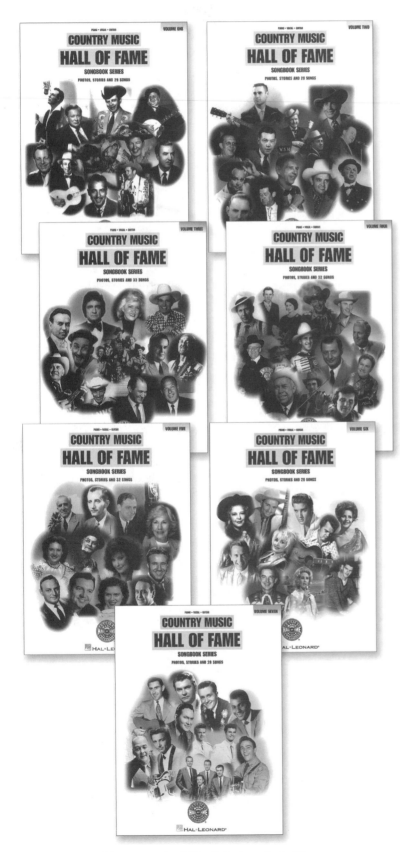

VOLUME 1

Features Jimmie Davis, Tennessee Ernie Ford, Minnie Pearl, Jim Reeves, Hank Williams, a others. Includes photos, stories, and 29 songs, including: The Ballad of Davy Crockett • C the Circle Be Unbroken • Deep in the Heart of Texas • Jambalaya (On the Bayou) • May Bird of Paradise Fly Up Your Nose • Mule Train • Rocky Top • You Are My Sunshine • Yo Cheatin' Heart • and more.

_____00313058 P/V/G ....$12.

VOLUME 2

Features Roy Acuff, Owen Bradley, Lester Flatt and Earl Scruggs, Tex Ritter, Merle Travis, B Wills, and more. 29 songs, including: Divorce Me C.O.D. • He Stopped Loving Her Today I'm Sorry • San Antonio Rose • Sixteen Tons • Wabash Cannon Ball • and more.

_____00313059 P/V/G ....$12.

VOLUME 3

Features Gene Autry, Johnny Cash, Roy Horton, Bill Monroe, Willie Nelson, Frances Prest Ernest Tubb, and other Hall of Famers. 33 songs, including: Always on My Mind • Folsom Pris Blues • (I Never Promised You A) Rose Garden • It Makes No Difference Now • Kentucky W • On the Road Again • Ring of Fire • Sugarfoot Rag • Tennessee Saturday Night • Tumbl Tumbleweeds • Walking the Floor Over You • and more.

_____00313060 P/V/G $12

VOLUME 4

Features Eddy Arnold, Chet Atkins, the Original Carter Family, Merle Haggard, Pee Wee Ki Hubert Long, Roger Miller, Floyd Tillman, and more. 32 songs, including: Bouquet of Ro • Dang Me • Green Green Grass of Home • Happy Trails • Heartbreak Hotel • If You've the Money (I've Got the Time) • John Henry • King of the Road • Mama Tried • Okie Fr Muskogee • Tennessee Waltz • Yakety Axe • and more.

_____00313061 P/V/G $12

VOLUME 5

Features Patsy Cline, Jim Denny, Connie B. Gay, Loretta Lynn, Marty Robbins, and others. songs, including: Blue Eyes Crying in the Rain • Coal Miner's Daughter • Crazy • 'Deed I • El Paso • I Fall to Pieces • The Long Black Veil • Pistol Packin' Mama • Ruby, Don't T Your Love to Town • You Ain't Woman Enough • and more.

_____00313062 P/V/G $12

VOLUME 6

PHOTOS, STORIES AND 28 SONGS

A wonderful treasury of country music legends, complete with photos and bios of each of featured honorees. This volume showcases Hall of Fame inductees Johnny Bond, Har Howard, Brenda Lee, Buck Owens, Dolly Parton, Elvis Presley, Ray Price, Conway Twitty, Ci Walker and Tammy Wynette. Includes photos, bios, and 28 songs from the artists: Above Beyond • Act Naturally • Coat of Many Colors • D-I-V-O-R-C-E • Don't Be Cruel (To a He That's True) • Heartaches by the Number • Heartbreak Hotel • Hello Darlin' • Hot Lincoln • I Will Always Love You • I'm Sorry • I've Got a Tiger by the Tail • It's Only M Believe • Love Me Tender • Release Me • Stand by Your Man • Tomorrow Never Come You Don't Know Me • and more.

_____00313202 P/V/G $12

VOLUME 7

PHOTOS, STORIES AND 28 SONGS

This volume features Country Music Hall of Fame honorees Bill Anderson, The Eve Brothers, Don Gibson, Waylon Jennings, The Jordanaires, Don Law, Sam Phillips, W Pierce, Charlie Pride and Faron Young. Includes photos and bios of each, plus 28 g representative songs: All I Have to Offer You Is Me • Ballad of a Teenage Queen • Battle New Orleans • Big Bad John • Blue Suede Shoes • Bye Bye Love • Cathy's Clown • Gambler • A Good Hearted Woman • Great Balls of Fire • Hello Walls • Hey Joe • I C Stop Loving You • Is Anybody Going to San Antone • Kiss an Angel Good Mornin' • Mam Don't Let Your Babies Grow Up to Be Cowboys • Oh, Lonesome Me • Waterloo • When I Be Loved • and more.

_____00313203 P/V/G $12

FOR MORE INFORMATION, SEE YOUR LOCAL MUSIC DEALER, OR WRITE TO:

HAL•LEONARD® CORPORATION

7777 W. BLUEMOUND RD. P.O. BOX 13819 MILWAUKEE, WI 53213

Visit Hal Leonard Online at
www.halleonard.com

Prices, contents and availability subject to change without notice.

THE DEFINITIVE COLLECTIONS

These magnificent folios each feature a premier selection of songs. Each has outstanding piano/vocal arrangements showcased by beautiful full-color covers. Books are spiral-bound for convenience and longevity.

The Definitive Blues Collection

A massive collection of 96 blues classics. Songs include: Baby, Won't You Please Come Home • Basin Street Blues • Everyday (I Have the Blues) • Gloomy Sunday • I'm a Man • (I'm Your) Hoochie Coochie Man • Milk Cow Blues • Nobody Knows You When You're Down and Out • The Seventh Son • St. Louis Blues • The Thrill Is Gone • and more.
00311563 ....$29.95

The Definitive Broadway Collection

142 of the greatest show tunes ever compiled into one volume, including: Don't Cry for Me Argentina • Hello, Dolly! • I Dreamed a Dream • Lullaby of Broadway • Mack the Knife • Memory • Send in the Clowns • Somewhere • The Sound of Music • Sunrise, Sunset • Tomorrow • What I Did for Love • more.
00359570 ....$29.95

The Definitive Children's Collection

126 songs children know and love, including: Any Dream Will Do • Beauty and the Beast • Bingo • The Brady Bunch • The Candy Man • Do-Re-Mi • Eensy Weensy Spider • Hakuna Matata • It's a Small World • Kum Ba Yah • On Top of Spaghetti • Pop Goes the Weasel • Puff the Magic Dragon • The Rainbow Connection • Sesame Street Theme • Take Me Out to the Ball Game • Won't You Be My Neighbor? • and more!
00310460 ....$22.95

The Definitive Christmas Collection

An authoritative collection of 126 Christmas classics, including: Blue Christmas • The Chipmunk Song • The Christmas Song (Chestnuts Roasting) • Feliz Navidad • Frosty the Snow Man • Happy Hanukkah, My Friend • Happy Holiday • (There's No Place Like) Home for the Holidays • O Come, All Ye Faithful • Rudolph, the Red-Nosed Reindeer • Tennessee Christmas • more!
00311602 ....$29.95

The Definitive Classical Collection

129 selections of favorite classical piano pieces and instrumental and operatic literature transcribed for piano. Features music by Johann Sebastian Bach, Ludwig van Beethoven, Georges Bizet, Johannes Brahms, Frederic Chopin, Claude Debussy, George Frideric Handel, Felix Mendelssohn, Johann Pachelbel, Franz Schubert, Johann Strauss, Jr., Pyotr Il'yich Tchaikovsky, Richard Wagner, and many more!
00310772 ....$29.95

The Definitive Country Collection

A must-own collection of 101 country classics, including: Coward of the County • Crazy • Daddy Sang Bass • Forever and Ever, Amen • Friends in Low Places • God Bless the U.S.A. • Grandpa (Tell Me About the Good Old Days) • Help Me Make It Through the Night • I Was Country When Country Wasn't Cool • I'm Not Lisa • I've Come to Expect It from You • I've Cried My Last Tear for You • Luckenbach, Texas • Make the World Go Away • Mammas Don't Let Your Babies Grow Up to Be Cowboys • Okie from Muskogee • Tennessee Flat Top Box • Through the Years • Where've You Been • and many more.
00311555 ....$29.95

The Definitive Dixieland Collection

Over 70 Dixieland classics, including: Ain't Misbehavin' • Alexander's Ragtime Band • Basin Street Blues • Bill Bailey, Won't You Please Come Home? • Dinah • Do You Know What It Means to Miss New Orleans? • I Ain't Got Nobody • King Porter Stomp • Shreveport Stomp • When the Saints Go Marching In • and more.
00311575 ....$29.95

The Definitive Hymn Collection

An amazing collection of over 200 treasured hymns, including: Abide with Me • All Glory, Laud and Honor • All Things Bright and Beautiful • At the Cross • Battle Hymn of the Republic • Be Thou My Vision • Blessed Assurance • Church in the Wildwood • Higher Ground • How Firm a Foundation • In the Garden • Just As I Am • A Mighty Fortress Is Our God • Nearer, My God, to Thee • The Old Rugged Cross • Rock of Ages • Sweet By and By • Were You There? • and more.
00310773 ....$29.95

The Definitive Jazz Collection

90 of the greatest jazz songs ever. including: Ain't Misbehavin' • All the Things You Are • Birdland • Body and Soul • Girl from Ipanema • The Lady Is a Tramp • Midnight Sun • Moonlight in Vermont • Night and Day • Skylark • Stormy Weather • Sweet Georgia Brown.
00359571 ....$29.95

The Definitive Love Collection

Over 100 sentimental favorites! Includes: All I Ask of You • Can't Help Falling in Love • Endless Love • The Glory of Love • Here and Now • I've Got My Love to Keep Me Warm • Isn't It Romantic? • Love Me Tender • Save the Best for Last • So in Love • Somewhere Out There • Unforgettable • When I Fall in Love • more.
00311681 ....$29.95

The Definitive Movie Collection

A comprehensive collection of over 100 songs that set the moods for movies, including: Alfie • Beauty and the Beast • Blue Velvet • Can You Feel the Love Tonight • Easter Parade • Endless Love • Forrest Gump Suite • Theme from Jurassic Park • One Tin Soldier • The Rainbow Connection • Someday My Prince Will Come • Under the Sea • Up Where We Belong • and more.
00311705 ....$29.95

The Definitive Rock 'n' Roll Collection

A classic collection of the best songs from the early rock 'n' roll years – 1955-1968. 95 songs, including: Barbara Ann • Chantilly Lace • Dream Lover • Duke of Earl • Earth Angel • Great Balls of Fire • Louie, Louie • Rock Around the Clock • Ruby Baby • Runaway • (Seven Little Girls) Sitting in the Back Seat • Stay • Surfin' U.S.A. • Wild Thing • Woolly Bully • and more.
00490195 ....$29.95